HOLY ROMANCE

7 Week Bible Study for Couples

DAVID AND KIMBERLY
SOESBEE

This is my beloved and this is my friend.

- Song of Solomon 5:16

Table of Contents

Introduction

Emotion Commotion

Satisfaction and boredom. Adoration and anger. Joy and sorrow. Admiration and disgust. Romance and contempt.

These are just some of the emotions you can expect to experience during your marriage.

"Boredom? Anger? Disgust?" you ask. "Even contempt?" What kind of marriage is that?

An honest one.

In the 1970s, psychologist Dr. Paul Ekman studied how facial expressions change when people experience emotions. He focused on six core emotions all humans have. At their basic level, these are happiness, sadness, fear, disgust, anger, and surprise[1]. Identifying the reasons behind our emotions and exactly how emotions are generated is terribly complex. They surface following stimulative responses that occur in the limbic system of the brain. Interestingly, the same stimulus does not always evoke the same emotive response; emotions vary greatly from person to person, making them subjective. The same experience might cause a person to have a reaction that appears highly logical to one observer and completely irrational to another. Why are there such disparities? How something will affect a person depends on on learned behaviors, cultural differences, and the uniquely personal experiences that define us.

Dr. Ekman explains it this way: "Emotions are a process, a particular kind of automatic appraisal influenced by our evolutionary and personal past, in which we sense that something important to our welfare is occurring, and a set of psychological changes and emotional behaviors begins to deal with the situation."

Emotions contribute greatly to our individuality and how we are perceived by others. And to make it even more multifaceted, a recent scientific study out of the Department of Psychology at the University of California, Berkeley identified twenty-seven distinct categories, or classifications, of human emotions[2].

Twenty-seven categories! That is a lot to process. The bottom line is our emotions are uniquely ours, and often the words and behaviors we choose to express our emotions don't accurately convey what is happening inside as we experience them. One thing we can grasp, however, is that emotions contribute greatly to how we process and react to the world around us.

Therefore, we can confidently say that you cannot live with someone every single day of your life "till-death-do-you-part" without experiencing the entire spectrum that lies within the categories of human emotions. It's not possible! Life is made up of both positive and negative experiences. Those in the covenant relationship of marriage will see them all. For better or for worse.

As couples prepare for marriage, they know in theory there will be good days and bad days. However, having this knowledge does not prepare you for how to deal with them. Couples are not equipped to handle the vast array of human emotional experiences another person will show in a lifetime.

Think about how you feel inside after having a bad day or when a huge problem comes up. The emotions in that moment may not have anything to do with your spouse, but what often happens is we project our negative feelings onto our partners, and they become linked with that negativity. Your reactions elicit reactions and emotions in your mate, and before you know it, you are fighting, and you aren't sure why.

Though we can't stop negative emotions from happening, we can control how we behave in response.

A hard, sad fact is Christian marriages fail every day. Divorce rates do not look vastly different between those who attend church and those who do not[3]. And leaving a spouse doesn't always mean divorce. Emotionally, relationally, and intellectually, Christian men and women leave one another every day. On the heels of a negative emotional experience, a little hurt turns into a few biting words. One night of rolling over without the goodnight kiss turns into two, then into a week. Sex is replaced with television or phone apps. Pretty soon one spouse hardly notices or cares if the other is even home when he or she goes to bed. There is a sigh of relief when the other person leaves instead of a longing for their return.

We blame work. We blame kids. We blame our own poor health. We blame the busyness of life. We blame problems. And in our excuses, we give ourselves permission to stop caring. We give permission for the negative emotions to linger. Once that permission is granted, anything goes.

This must stop.

Our experience in writing this book does not come because we have it all together. Our kids can attest that we have *all* the emotions going on—and some that even Berkeley may not have seen! But what we also have is a commitment at the end of the day to the Holy Romance to which God has called us. It trumps all human experience. It cleanses us from past mistakes. It woos us back from the grave to a place of love. God called us first into His Holy Romance, and it is only through His love that we can manage to make better choices in this emotionally turbulent world. Living out the love of Christ in a marriage relationship involves making decisions that align with God's word.

Three Truths

You might be thinking, "That would be great if only

my husband..." Or "It would be a lot easier to follow God's word if my wife would just..." If your mind went to that place, let us stop you right there. Your obedience to God's word is not dependent on the behavior of another person. This is a foundational truth to living out God's will for your life, and it needs to be addressed in your own heart before you can experience growth in your marriage. A marriage based on blame or waiting for another person to change is doomed to fail. Decide before we begin that you will lay aside any temptation to blame another as a hindrance to your personal growth.

A second truth to understand as we embark on a journey to better understand God's plan for marriage is to know this: Satan hates your marriage. 1 Peter 5:8 instructs that we are to: *"Be of sober spirit, be on the alert. Your adversary, the devil, prowls around like a roaring lion, seeking someone to devour."*

Nothing would make Satan more pleased than to see your marriage fall apart. But he can't devour you if you don't give him an entry point. We will talk more about this in subsequent Scripture study. For now, as you begin this study, pray daily for protection. Pray for the wisdom to know when Satan's lies are trying to worm their way into your brain. Call it out and squash it when he is trying to convince you that any lack of spiritual growth is your spouse's problem, not yours.

Finally, the third foundational truth is a pretty big deal, and it's perhaps the most important thing you can do for yourself. We live in a culture that is at the same time obsessed with love and yet starved for the kind of love that changes lives for the better: God's love. But here's the thing: Without the Holy Spirit, it is *impossible* to love others with Jesus's love. Why? Because you don't have it in you. When you accept Jesus as your Savior and make the decision to give Him Lordship over your life by repenting of your sins and believing in Him alone for salvation, the

Holy Spirit takes up residence inside you. He brings the power of God and the love of Christ to a place that was void and perishing—your soul.

Hebrews 11:6 reads: *"Without faith, it is impossible to please God."* This faith-filled chapter of Hebrews is recounting the belief that God is who He says He is, as demonstrated by the heroes of the Old Testament. At the end of that chapter and beginning of the next we are told that God has provided something even better for us! We learn that Jesus is the author and perfecter of that faith! Without Him, we simply are not connected to the Father.

If you are beginning this study and have not accepted Jesus as your Savior and as Lord of your life, please don't give up or decide this isn't for you. God speaks to all people, giving the opportunity to learn the truth of His character. Give it a chance and know, the love we speak of can be yours today through the power of the Holy Spirit.

This Study

Even once you have the Holy Spirit, there are things that can be barriers to loving ourselves and loving others. These barriers can block our marriages from thriving in the holy romance that God desires us to have, with Him first and then with our spouse. We need to identify and bring those things to God for destruction. That is the focus of this study. We will openly address decisions you can make that will have a profound impact on your marriage.

Lesson Structure

There are 7 lessons in this book. Ideally, you and your spouse will complete one lesson in the course of a week's time, then meet together with your small group and review your completed lessons. If your small group has a designated leader, the leader will find helpful advice for running a successful group beginning on page 107 of this study.

After each Lesson Introduction is a **Spicy Meatball**. The Spicy Meatball is a bold statement to which you may find you have a fleshly reaction. It relates to the key decision to be made in that lesson. Be warned! Spicy Meatballs can be difficult to digest.

Pay attention to how the Spicy Meatball makes you feel. What is your initial reaction to it? You'll want to discuss your initial thoughts in your group time, and identify how those thoughts change after you complete the rest of the lesson. When you embrace the biblical truth of the Spicy Meatball, you will experience growth.

Me Time offers you the space for independent Scripture study. It is time we pray will be used by the Holy Spirit to speak to you through God's word. We've left plenty of room for you to write in this book, so grab a pen and go for it! Once both you and your spouse have completed Me Time for the week, you are ready for...

We Time. Carve 30 minutes in your week to complete the We Time reflections together. We Time involves life application, discussion starters, prayer leading, and opportunity to grow closer through transparency. Make the decision to let your We Time be free of judgments and free from ridicule. As you will see, your marriage relationship should be the safest place outside of God's love.

The **Journal Reflection** is a personal exercise with no right or wrong answers. Complete it at any time, whenever you are ready.

God's Holy Romance

In contemporary use, the word romance is synonymous with love, affection, and passion. It is both a noun and a verb.

As a verb, it is descriptive of actions designed to spark a particular emotional reaction from another. It involves courting or wooing behaviors for the purpose of generating love feelings in another. We don't "romance" our friends. We don't "romance" our family members. We romance someone with whom we want an intimate, passionate, love-relationship.

As a noun, the word romance refers to that relational exchange. It is the manifestation of the feelings that acting romantically will bring.

God pursues us romantically in that He wants to have an intimate, loving, passionate emotional connection to you. He wants to occupy first place in your life, and He wants you to seek Him with passion and commitment. He pursues us because we are important to Him.

The only human person who is to get your romantic pursuits is your spouse. Yes, we date, we court, and we woo one another before we are married. You may romantically pursue different people before finding someone with whom you want to say "I do." But once that commitment is made, romantic love is reserved for your husband or wife. No one else.

Before you begin Lesson 1, turn to page 105. There you will find a pre-study questionnaire. Take a few minutes to privately complete the questions. We will revisit them after the final lesson.

We may not know your names, but know we are praying for you to experience God's holy romance first and foremost more deeply in your life, so that you are overflowing with the love of Christ for your spouse.

Lesson 1
The Decision to be Different

Lesson Introduction

We have before us a two-fold, radical challenge:

1. We are to be unconditionally committed to Christ.
2. We are to be unconditionally committed to each other.

As simple as that sounds, it's deeply profound... and often difficult, too![4] Unfortunately, the decisions we make in response to our emotions can construct barriers between ourselves and the people we love, making it tough to live out these commitments. Once those barriers are in place, it's going to take some work to get through them.

In the 1976 boxing movie *Rocky*, there is a scene near the end where the young, underdog fighter is in the battle of his life against the champion of the world, Apollo Creed. Rocky's face is battered, bruised, bloody. His eyes are swollen so badly that he cannot see. His energy is all but depleted, and his muscles spent from giving everything within to surviving this fight.

In the brief reprise between rounds, he goes to his corner, where his support team awaits. He begs his faithful coach Mickey to help him see. He chokes out the famous line, "Cut me, Mick." They slice his eye to drain the blood, doing all they can to ready Rocky to continue the fight.

The corner man plays a critical role in the success or failure of any fighter. Encouragement, support, first aid, water, a place for rest, motivation... the corner man gives whatever the fighter needs to summon the bravery and strength to continue the fight.

We paint this picture because now we want you to think of your spouse in the boxing ring. Put your spouse in the role of Rocky. Picture your spouse wearing Rocky's satin boxing shorts and his black boxing gloves. Got the image?

Now put yourself in the ring with your spouse.

Where are you in the picture? Are you Apollo Creed? Or are you Mickey? Are you wearing the other set of boxing gloves, facing your spouse as an opponent? Or are you the corner man?

We are to be our spouse's corner man. Every day. Every time. Whether we feel disappointment or delight. Whether we feel happiness or anger. You are on the same side.

That doesn't mean you have to agree with everything your spouse says. Rocky and Mickey didn't always agree. But they knew without a doubt that even in disagreement, each had the good of the other at the heart of the intent. That knowledge allowed them to disagree without it damaging the core of the relationship. So when they faced the fights of the world, they were still on the same side.

The world will tell you that men and women will always be at odds. You've heard the term "The Battle of the Sexes." It is not to be that way in marriage.

The Spicy Meatball...
If your marriage is going to please God, you must operate under different principles than the world.

1. What questions come to mind when you read the above statement? How does it make you feel?

Me Time

Read Mark 10:35-45

35 James and John, the two sons of Zebedee, came up to Jesus, saying to Him, "Teacher, we want You to do for us whatever we ask of You." 36 And He said to them, "What do you want Me to do for you?" 37 They said to Him, "Grant that we may sit, one on Your right and one on Your left, in Your glory." 38 But Jesus said to them, "You do not know what you are asking. Are you able to drink the cup that I drink, or to be baptized with the baptism with which I am baptized?" 39 They said to Him, "We are able." And Jesus said to them, "The cup that I drink you shall drink; and you shall be baptized with the baptism with which I am baptized. 40 But to sit on My right or on My left is not Mine to give; but it is for those for whom it has been prepared."

41 Hearing this, the other ten began to feel indignant with James and John. 42 Calling them to Himself, Jesus said to them, "You know that those who are recognized as rulers of the Gentiles domineer over them; and their people in high position exercise authority over them. 43 But it is not this way among you; rather, whoever wants to become prominent among you shall be your servant; 44 and whoever wants to be first among you shall be slave of all. 45 For even the Son of Man did not come to be served, but to serve, and to give His life as a ransom for many."

2. What did James and John ask of Jesus?

Not long before this request, James and John, along with Peter, were privy to something the other disciples were not. In your Bible, back up a chapter and read Mark 9:1-8. List below some of the miraculous things that happened in those verses.

3. How might James and John have felt about what they saw?

Have you ever witnessed something that left you speechless? James, John, and Peter heard the voice of God Himself! They alone were granted this glimpse into the intimate relationship between Jesus, Elijah, and Moses, capped off with a word from God. James and John's response? They want in on the glory! Let's see how Jesus responds to their request.

4. What does Jesus say in Mark 10:38?

5. What is the "cup" that Jesus is referring to?

Jesus knew the suffering He would endure. Jesus knew His death was required to conquer sin. The others had not grasped it yet.

6. Does Jesus appear angry in His response to James and John? Reread Mark 10:39,40. What do you think?

Jesus's response appears instructive. He makes no false promises. He clearly states: "You will, indeed, suffer, but the seats at my right and left are not Mine to give." The ten disciples have quite a different emotional reaction to James and John's request. Read Mark 10:41.

7. Look up the word "indignant" in your dictionary. Write the definition below:

8. The Greek word used in this verse is **aganakteó**. It means "to grieve much, to be greatly afflicted, to be much displeased.[5]" Why were the ten so angry at James and John's request? What initiated this emotional reaction?

9. Jesus responds immediately. He calls all of them over, and in Mark 10:42, Jesus describes characteristics of those who are rulers over Gentiles; in other words, those seeking worldly domination. How does Jesus describe them?

10. Read Mark 10:43. Write the first sentence of that verse below.

Mark 10:43 and Matthew 20:26 both begin with a phrase that we want you to remember when you are tempted to let your emotions get the better of you. We are going to list it as written in a few different translations.

NIV - "Not so with you."

NASB - "It is not this way among you."

NKJV - "Yet it shall not be so among you."

A follower of Christ cannot operate with the same motives as one who seeks to have power and authority from a worldly view. It is the same in our marriages. When our emotions threaten to get the better of us in marriage, we have to take a step back and listen for the voice of Jesus telling us, "It is not to be this way among you!"

11. Look up each of the verses listed below. Each presents a characteristic of either someone seeking worldly domination or someone who is a Christ follower. Write the qualities in the correct column of the chart.

Verse	Worldly domination	Christ follower
Philippians 2:3, 4		
Romans 14:10		
1 Corinthians 4:1, 2		
Mark 9:35		
Matthew 23:13		

12. When Jesus says, "Not so with you," specifically, how is he saying that you are NOT to act?

♥ We Time

Read the following verses together with your spouse:

Ephesians 5:22-33

22 Wives, subject yourselves to your own husbands, as to the Lord. 23 For the husband is the head of the wife, as Christ also is the head of the church, He Himself being the Savior of the body. 24 But as the church is subject to Christ, so also the wives ought to be to their husbands in everything.

25 Husbands, love your wives, just as Christ also loved the church and gave Himself up for her, 26 so that He might sanctify her, having cleansed her by the washing of water with the word, 27 that He might present to Himself the church in all her glory, having no spot or wrinkle or any such thing; but that she would be holy and blameless. 28 So husbands also ought to love their own wives as their own bodies. He who loves his own wife loves himself; 29 for no one ever hated his own flesh, but nourishes and cherishes it, just as Christ also does the church, 30 because we are parts of His body. 31 For this reason a man shall leave his father and his mother and be joined to his wife, and the two shall become one flesh. 32 This mystery is great; but I am speaking with reference to Christ and the church. 33 Nevertheless, as for you individually, each husband is to love his own wife the same as himself, and the wife must see to it that she respects her husband.

In your Me Time time, we acknowledged the difference between worldly dominion and Christ's dominion.

To sum it up: Leadership done Christ's way embodies an attitude of servanthood. Leadership done the world's way involves selfishness and control.

13. Consider the verses from Ephesians 5 through the lens of what you read in your Me Time. In these verses, there are 8 uses of the preposition "*as*". For example, in verse 22 we read the phrase "*as to the Lord*." Highlight or underline each phrase that begins with "*as___*."

14. What do you notice about these prepositional phrases that begin with the word "*as*"?

Do you see that the word "*as*" is used to provide comparisons? Ultimately we are to treat our spouse **as** Christ treats us. How has Christ treated us? Read these verses from Philippians 2:5-8:

5 Have this attitude in yourselves which was also in Christ Jesus, 6 who, as He already existed in the form of God, did not consider equality with God something to be grasped, 7 but emptied Himself by taking the form of a bond-servant and being born in the likeness of men. 8 And being found in appearance as a man, He humbled Himself by becoming obedient to the point of death: death on a cross.

15. Which words in these verses describe Christ's attitude?

16. List below ways you have seen your spouse treat you with an attitude of servanthood. It can be as simple as "he/she stopped at the store last week and picked up milk."

17. Now, identify ways you can treat your spouse with an attitude of servanthood in the upcoming week. If this is difficult for you, start with **one** thing that can show an attitude of servanthood.

18. Are there specific situations you find yourself in as a couple that make it difficult to show servanthood to one another? What is one small thing you can do to address this?

Journal Reflection

The disciples became angry at John and James for asking for something they didn't think they deserved. Because we live in an emotionally turbulent world, there will be times when you feel indignant with your spouse. What have you noticed from this week's study that can help you in those times?

Closing Thoughts

Making the decision to be your spouse's corner man is critical for your marriage to reflect God's Holy Romance. Remember, the corner man is a servant to the fighter. They serve by giving what is needed, when it is needed most. Every day, the world is going to throw punches at our spouse. If you decide ahead of time not to join in the fight but to serve in the recovery, your marriage will grow. And when both spouses make the commitment to be the other's corner man, you become a team with little room for Satan to get a foothold into.

Lesson 2
The Decision to Pray

Lesson Introduction

Reflect on the past week and your own attitude of servanthood. What did you notice about servanthood and marriage?

Growth is a process. You won't get it right every time. Old habits will surface. Unloving words will come from your own lips when difficult emotions are stirred. However, you will notice in increasing measures you are able to put into practice that which God teaches you.

This week we are going to focus on the decision for spiritual growth. It begins with prayer. If you desire God to refine you, then ask Him to do it! He will. Ask Him to help you hate your sinful ways. Ask Him to help you respond to your spouse with His love. Ask Him to show you how you can love *as Christ loves the church.*

Pursue Him and He will disclose Himself more and more to you. There is an awesome promise found in Philippians 2:13: *"It is God who is at work in you, both to desire and to work for His good pleasure."*

Change Begins with Prayer

It is easy to love someone when they are acting loveable. When your husband vacuums the entire house and buys your favorite brand of ice cream. When your wife gives a shoulder massage before bed after a long day. When the toddler is up early on a Saturday and your spouse says, "Stay in bed, I'll get up with him." Woo! Bring on the feelings of love! But as we've discussed, marriage will also see the feelings that are not so warm and fuzzy. Times of annoyance, frustration, even disgust. Yet, we are called to be servants and love anyway. So how do we do it?

God has wisely given us a formula to prepare ourselves for each and every human emotion that comes our way. It is found in 1 Thessalonians 5:16-18:

16 Rejoice always, 17 pray without ceasing, 18 in everything give thanks; for this is the will of God for you in Christ Jesus.

Can this process really help change your heart when your spouse has said or done something hurtful? You may not yet believe it, but the answer is a resounding, "Yes!" God would not instruct us with words like "always," "without ceasing," and "in everything," unless He knew we could handle it. He is the key ingredient in the formula.

When we come together in marriage, our union is new and fresh, but we come bringing behaviors and emotions that have been built throughout the course of our lives. If our childhoods have been difficult, if we've suffered at the hands of someone else, if we've been let down or hurt in other relationships, we bring our coping mechanisms from our past with us. Those coping mechanisms are often the things that drive a wedge between couples.

Consider this real-life example:

Mike had a rough childhood. Dysfunctional family, a father who was not present, he spent a lot of time alone, ran with the wrong crowd, and learned how to get what he needed by fighting for it or by deceiving others.

Amy grew up in a single-mom environment. Her mother was bitter when it came to men and relationships, and demonstrated criticism and a condescending spirit in most situations. Amy's previous love-relationship was unfaithful and she has difficulty trusting others.

Amy and Mike both accepted Christ as adults. But they come to their marriage with coping mechanisms and learned examples of how to treat others borne from their youth. Mike's default to not getting what he wants is to get angry and demanding. He goes into fight-mode quickly. Amy responds with criticism and mistrust. When threatened, she clings to her own superiority.

What does prayer look like for them? Our human default is to pray for the other person to change. Mike might pray that Amy would come off her high-horse and stop doubting his love. Amy might pray that Mike would learn to control his temper and stop being so mean. And those aren't bad things to pray for! But if the *only* thing you pray for is that the other person will change, you are missing an important piece of the puzzle.

Amy began to pray that the Lord would show her places where she was too critical. She began to pray that she would have a loving response instead of getting defensive when she felt threatened emotionally.

Mike began to pray that God would show him ways to express himself more calmly. He began to pray for ways that he could build Amy up and show her that she can trust him. He began to pray for a change in his own heart.

You see, the only person you have control over is you. You can't decide for someone else to change. You can pray for it, but you also must pray for your own emotional responses to change. You must pray that when faced with a choice to either respond with love or to join in the battle, God will show you the loving response.

This week's study will equip you with Scripture to support this decision.

The Spicy Meatball...
If your only prayer is for someone else to
change, you will always struggle to be at peace.

1. What are your thoughts as you consider this statement?

Me Time

Our Me Time begins in Acts 16. Paul, along with Silas and Timothy, are travelling throughout the Mediterranean region. On this journey, they were led by directives from the apostles in Jerusalem (v. 4) and guided by the Holy Spirit (vs. 6-9). As men and women showed their hearts open to the message, Paul and the team preached the way of salvation. Many were healed. While they were in Philippi, a slave girl, who made a lot of money for her masters as a fortune teller, began to follow them, crying out loudly after them. She persisted in this for many days.

We learn in verse 18 that this girl "greatly annoyed" Paul with her actions. In his annoyance, Paul commanded the evil spirit to leave the girl immediately, and it did. This impulsive reaction on Paul's part brought instant trouble on Paul and Silas.

The masters were furious that a source of their revenue was gone. As a result, they had Paul and Silas beaten and imprisoned. That is the setting for this passage.

Read Acts 16:23-30:
23 *When they had struck them with many blows, they threw them into prison, commanding the jailer to guard them securely;* 24 *and he, having received such a command, threw them into the inner prison and fastened their feet in the*

stocks.

25 *But about midnight Paul and Silas were praying and singing hymns of praise to God, and the prisoners were listening to them; 26 and suddenly there came a great earthquake, so that the foundations of the prison house were shaken; and immediately all the doors were opened and everyone's chains were unfastened. 27 When the jailer awoke and saw the prison doors opened, he drew his sword and was about to kill himself, supposing that the prisoners had escaped. 28 But Paul cried out with a loud voice, saying, "Do not harm yourself, for we are all here!" 29 And he called for lights and rushed in, and trembling with fear he fell down before Paul and Silas, 30 and after he brought them out, he said, "Sirs, what must I do to be saved?"*

2. What were Paul and Silas doing right before the earthquake happened?[6]

3. Who else was present?

4. What happened to the prison after the earthquake?

5. What was the jailer's initial reaction? Were his initial assumptions correct?

6. What was his response when he saw that everyone was still there?

Before we digest these verses further, let's flip over to Acts 12. Read verses 1-11:

1 Now about that time Herod the king laid hands on some who belonged to the church, to do them harm. 2 And he had James the brother of John executed with a sword. 3 When he saw that it pleased the Jews, he proceeded to arrest Peter as well. (Now these were the days of Unleavened Bread.) 4 When he had arrested him, he put him in prison, turning him over to four squads of soldiers to guard him, intending only after the Passover to bring him before the people. 5 So Peter was kept in the prison, but prayer for him was being made to God intensely by the church.

6 On the very night when Herod was about to bring him forward, Peter was sleeping between two soldiers, bound with two chains, and guards in front of the door were watching over the prison. 7 And behold, an angel of the Lord suddenly stood near Peter, and a light shone in the cell; and he struck Peter's side and woke him, saying, "Get up quickly." And his chains fell off his hands. 8 And the angel said to him, "Put on your belt and strap on your sandals." And he did so. And he said to him, "Wrap your cloak around you and follow me." 9 And he went out and continued to follow, and yet he did not know that what was being done by the angel was real, but thought he was seeing a vision. 10 Now when they had passed the first and second guard, they came to the iron gate that leads into the city, which opened for them by itself; and they went out and went along one street, and immediately the angel departed from him. 11 When Peter

came to himself, he said, "Now I know for sure that the Lord
has sent forth His angel and rescued me from the hand of
Herod and from all that the Jewish people were expecting."

7. God allowed Peter's chains to fall off miraculously to
deliver him from prison. Paul and Silas certainly would
have known about Peter's miracle. They may have thought
the earthquake was their chance to be freed, too. None of
us would have faulted Paul and Silas had they taken the
opportunity to escape. But they stayed put. How do you
think they knew God wanted them to remain in that
difficult situation?

8. Do you think that the answer you gave for question 2
had anything to do with Paul and Silas knowing how to
respond in the earthquake? Explain.

Read 1 Corinthians 2:14-16:
14 But a natural man does not accept the things of the Spirit
of God, for they are foolishness to him; and he cannot
understand them, because they are spiritually appraised.
15 But he who is spiritual appraises all things, yet he himself
is appraised by no one. 16 For who has known the mind of
the LORD, that he will instruct him? But we have the mind of
Christ.

9. Whose mind do you think Paul and Silas were linked
with at the moment they were in the prison?

Paul and Silas were led by the Holy Spirit. Acts 16:25
told us they were praying and singing hymns in the
presence of the other prisoners. They abided in Christ,
even in their imprisonment! As such, God showed them
what to do. They did not do the thing that was in the best
interest for themselves; they did what was in the best
interest for the jailer! He got saved! The human mind
would have told them to get away when given the
opportunity. The Holy Spirit led them to stay. See how
powerful it can be to rejoice, pray, and give thanks in all
circumstances?

Building a consistent, intentional prayer routine, both
individually and with your spouse, will ready you for any
situation. And if you need two more reasons, they are "peace
and plans."

Peace: Philippians 2:6,7
*6 Do not be anxious about anything, but in everything by
prayer and pleading with thanksgiving let your requests be
made known to God. 7 And the **peace** of God, which
surpasses all comprehension, will guard your hearts and
minds in Christ Jesus.*

Plans: Jeremiah 29:11
*11 'For I know the **plans** that I have for you,' declares the
Lord, 'plans for prosperity and not for disaster, to give you a
future and a hope.'*

10. How would remaining connected to the One who holds your future in His hands impact your relationships?

 **We Time**

For this lesson's We Time, we are going to explore several different prayer techniques that you and your spouse can practice together. If praying together is a new experience, it might seem awkward at first. The spiritual discipline of prayer is just that—a discipline. And any discipline becomes stronger the more you engage it. These are not the only ways to pray, they are simply a few that we think can be a powerful way to grow spiritually, individually and together.

Technique 1: Praying through Scripture
Reading Scripture and then praying it back to God is a powerful way to strengthen your faith. The psalms are structured well for this, however any passage of Scripture can be prayed back to God. Simply read a verse or section of verses aloud to the Lord and then pray to God to be sentient to the principles presented.

Here is an example from Psalm 141:1-4. The italicized verses are Scripture, the bolded words would be a prayer to God. We'll use the plural "we" in our prayer, as we hope you and your spouse will practice this together.

1 Lord, I call upon You; hurry to me!
Listen to my voice when I call to You!

Lord, thank You that when we call, You will answer. We know that You hear our voices.

2 May my prayer be counted as incense before You;
The raising of my hands as the evening offering.

Our prayers will rise as incense before you. We raise our hands in offering to You.

3 Set a guard, Lord, over my mouth;
Keep watch over the door of my lips.

Guard our words, Lord. Protect our mouths and what comes from our lips.

4 Do not incline my heart to any evil thing,
To practice deeds of wickedness
With people who do wrong;
And may I not taste their delicacies.

Do not let our attention turn to any evil things. Do not let us practice wickedness. Keep us from people who do wrong in your sight. Do not let us taste in their sinful desires. Amen.

It can help to have one spouse read the Scripture and the other pray. You can take turns in each role. Here are some Scriptures to practice with:

Psalm 1	Philippians 2	1 John 1
Psalm 28	2 Corinthians 4	1 John 3
Psalm 98	Herbrews 12	1 John 4

Technique 2: Prayer Journaling

Some people find that their minds wander when they pray silently. If this is you, fear not! Prayer journaling might be the answer. You can type or write your prayers to the Lord, and the act of writing can help you stay focused. The key is not to overthink what you are going to write. Ask the Holy Spirit to guide your hand. It might help to set a timer and just simply write for the entire time, writing a letter to the Lord. It can be to give thanks, to make supplication (asking Him for something), rejoicing for His character, praising Him for your salvation—there are no limits.

Let's practice together. Gather a pen and paper or open a document on your device on which you can type. Set a timer for two minutes. Our topic for this practice is to talk to God about **the good things happening in your marriage** or in your family.

Begin your writing: **Dear Jesus,**
Write for the entire two minutes without stopping. Try not to edit your thoughts, simply write. At the end of the two minutes, share what you wrote with your spouse.

Technique 3: Prayer Walk or Nature Reflection
Some find it powerful to observe God in nature. Go for a walk with your spouse. If it is difficult to schedule time to do this, start small. Begin with one lap, walking around your block or to the corner and back. Bring the kids if you need to. During your walk, observe the beauty around you. Thank God for what you see. Thank Him for your neighborhood and your home. Then turn your thanks to your spouse, naming specific characteristics for which you are grateful. Let each one of you take a turn expressing thanks for the other.

If you can do longer walks, here are some additional things you can pray for on your Prayer Walks.

your children	our nation
your children's future spouses	church leaders
your grandchildren	God-honoring friendships
lost family members	the lost in our world

Technique 4: Listening Prayer

Spend some time with your spouse, listening to God. You can begin by playing a worship song or a favorite hymn or by reading a passage of Scripture. Then quiet yourselves. Hold hands. Close your eyes. Listen.

Express whatever comes to your heart. Ask God to reveal Himself to you and your spouse. Come without an agenda. It might help when you are finished to write down at least one of the things the Lord spoke to your heart during your listening time. Keeping a record of the Lord's faithfulness can be a powerful tool to return to when you are feeling low in spirit.

Let's practice. There is a version of "Majesty" done by Maranatha Music on YouTube that can be accessed with this link: https://youtu.be/SNnTFDNPT3U (Type it in your search bar). Sit in a quiet place across from or next to your spouse. Hold hands, close your eyes, and listen. Then express to the Lord what He lays on your heart.

Journal Reflection

What are some of the things that distract you and your spouse from being intentional about praying together? Are you willing to do whatever it takes to make praying with and for your spouse a priority?

Closing Thoughts

The decision to pray with and for your spouse is the beginning of all positive change to be experienced in your marriage.

Many relationship disappointments can be avoided if you don't just pray for someone else to change, but pray for God to do a radical work in your own heart. Healing and restoration of brokenness is possible. It begins with prayer.

Lesson 3
The Decision to be Faithful

Lesson Introduction

As we write this, the year is 2022. We are more than two years into the COVID 19 pandemic. Whether we are "post pandemic" or not is a topic up for debate. We are certainly not recovered. Our political climate in America is chaotic and reckless. The educational gap between where our students should be and where they are is wide. Divorce rates[7], suicide rates, and numbers of domestic abuse cases are up.

Moreover, studies are finding that the social isolation, anxiety, fear of contagion, uncertainty, chronic stress, and economic difficulties in families are leading to the development or exacerbation of depressive, anxiety, substance use, and other psychiatric disorders.[8]

To top it off, church attendance is down and, according to a March 2020 article by *Psychology Today*, pornography usage has increased since the pandemic began.[9] Hear it again: More people are saturating themselves in pornography than ever before.

The statistics in all categories are grim.

For all of the reasons listed above, it is more important than ever to remain faithful to your marriage. Remaining faithful is a result of the small, day-to-day decisions about what you do, what you look at, who you spend time with, where you go, and the trains of thought you entertain.

Do you know anyone who just seems to be able to get more done in a day than you do? How is it possible when we all operate within the same 24-hour constraint? Why do some people seem to be more engaged, more "on it," more active, more organized? Well, time management definitely plays a role in productivity, but we want you to consider that management of one's emotional energy is also a key factor. How much you will get done and the quality of your relationships are impacted by how you decide to use your emotional energy. One book on the topic suggests: "the number of hours in a day is fixed, but the quantity and quality of energy available to us are not. It is our most precious resource."[10]

How you use your emotional energy throughout the day will impact the capacity you have for your spouse. But we want to frame this chapter around the decision to be faithful. Specifically, let's talk about romantic and sexual faithfulness.

Faithfulness is a quality that encompasses fidelity, loyalty, reliability, and the idea of allegiance. Faithfulness in marriage is so important to God, He listed it among the Ten Commandments. Exodus 20:14: *"You shall not commit adultery."* Shall. Not. The Bible verses from Ephesians 5 that we studied in Lesson 1 demonstrate that husband and wife are to treat each other as Christ does the church. Jesus is faithful to His church *(1 Corinthians 1:9, 1 Thessalonians 5:24)*.

In this lesson's study, we are not going to focus on whether or not faithfulness is needed; we hope you come into this with the agreement that faithfulness is the desired goal. What we will focus on are the things that prevent us from being faithful—red flags that perhaps Satan is gaining a foothold in your marriage that could lead to infidelity if not put in check. The decision to be unfaithful rarely happens all at once. It is a series of small decisions that culminates in abandonment of the marriage, either physically, emotionally, or spiritually.

Before we begin the Scripture study, we want to acknowledge that there are some couples reading this who may be working on restoring a marriage that was broken by unfaithfulness. There are some reading this who may be engaging in an extramarital affair that your spouse is unaware of (yes, this includes pornography). Dealing with past hurts and brokenness is a serious and difficult soul-healing process. You can't flip a switch and make the pain go away. What you can do is make the decision to immediately stop any behaviors in which you are giving your romantic and sexual energy away to someone who is not your spouse. You can make the decision to take your pain to Jesus when you feel it surfacing and ask Him to fill your heart with thoughts of love. Healing from infidelity is difficult, but it is possible when both spouses are willing to do the hard work of the soul. It is a work that can only be done with Jesus at the center.

Friend, you may be hurting because of something your spouse has done. Forgiveness may feel slow in coming. But hear us again, through Christ, it is possible. We ask that you stay with us in this process.

The Spicy Meatball...
Faithfulness is achieved through small, day-to-day decisions that prioritize your spouse and your marriage over other things.

1. What thoughts come to mind as you consider this statement?

Me Time

We are going to make a journey through the Old Testament, stopping at two impactful stories. Each has a lesson for us regarding the topic of fidelity. We will identify places in our own marriages where we may be giving the devil an opening. If you recognize yourself in any of these scenarios, count it as the Holy Spirit shining a light on your actions so that you can stop before it goes any further.

Faithfulness Lesson 1: Abram and Sarai - Genesis 16

The set up for this story is found in Genesis 15. God has made a promise to childless Abram that he will have an heir and that Abram's descendants will be as numerous as the stars. God has promised to give Abram land to possess and a future that will see his descendants struggle, but also prosper. God seals the deal by instituting a covenant to verify that all that He had spoken will come to be. It is pretty clear: Abram will have a son.

The problem comes when Sarai and Abram take matters into their own hands as to how this son will come to be. Let's read from Genesis 16:1-6:

1 Now Sarai, Abram's wife, had not borne him a child, but she had an Egyptian slave woman whose name was Hagar. 2 So Sarai said to Abram, "See now, the Lord has prevented me from bearing children. Please have relations with my slave woman; perhaps I will obtain children through her." And Abram listened to the voice of Sarai. 3 And so after Abram had lived ten years in the land of Canaan, Abram's wife Sarai took Hagar the Egyptian, her slave woman, and gave her to her husband Abram as his wife. 4 Then he had relations with Hagar, and she conceived; and when Hagar became aware that she had conceived, her mistress was despised in her sight. 5 So Sarai said to Abram, "May the wrong done to me

be upon you! I put my slave woman into your arms, but when
she saw that she had conceived, I was despised in her sight.
May the Lord judge between you and me." 6 But Abram said
to Sarai, "Look, your slave woman is in your power; do to her
what is good in your sight." So Sarai treated her harshly, and
she fled from her presence.

Abram and Sarai wanted the results of the promise
God made. However, God did not fulfill the promise for a
son in a timeframe that worked for them. They became
impatient, so Sarai took matters into her own hands to
make it happen. And look at the problems it caused!

2. Write the last sentence of verse 2:

Abram listened to Sarai's voice, not God's voice. Human
emotions drove everything that happened next.

3. How did Hagar feel once she knew she was pregnant?

4. Why might Hagar have felt that way about Sarai?

5. Did it work out the way Sarai envisioned? What
emotions does Abram show in verse 6?

Let's turn the questions inward.

6. Have you ever tried to manipulate a situation and it backfired on you? Explain.

7. Scripture indicates that the plan was initiated by Sarai. How could Abram have avoided the outcome?

Abram's first mistake was listening to Sarai, instead of listening to God. "But wait! Aren't I supposed to submit to my spouse?" you might ask. Not if what your spouse asks you to do goes against God's word. Going against God's word will always have repercussions.

Here is another Spicy Meatball for you: You can protect your marriage by avoiding counsel from those who do not profess Jesus as Lord and Savior. You might have some kind and good non-Christian people in your circle of friends, but if someone doesn't believe that God's way is the best way, the advice they will give you will come from the world's point of view. Doing things the world's way goes against doing things God's way. Facts.

8. If you have a disagreement or problem with your spouse, who do you turn to for help? Is that person a Christ-follower?

9. How can you avoid letting outside voices impact how you deal with situations in your marriage?

Faithfulness Lesson 2: David and Bathsheba - 2 Samuel 11

Our story in 2 Samuel 11 is one of adultery, cover-up, and murder. And it all begins with one man looking at something he should not. Let's begin with verses 1-5:

1 Then it happened in the spring, at the time when kings go out to battle, that David sent Joab and his servants with him and all Israel, and they destroyed the sons of Ammon and besieged Rabbah. But David stayed at Jerusalem.

2 Now when evening came David arose from his bed and walked around on the roof of the king's house, and from the roof he saw a woman bathing; and the woman was very beautiful in appearance. 3 So David sent and inquired about the woman. And one said, "Is this not Bathsheba, the daughter of Eliam, the wife of Uriah the Hittite?" 4 David sent messengers and took her, and when she came to him, he lay with her; and when she had purified herself from her uncleanness, she returned to her house. 5 The woman conceived; and she sent and told David, and said, "I am pregnant."

10. David was already married. After David noticed the beautiful woman bathing, what should he have done?

11. What is the danger of letting your eyes linger on attractive men or women who are not your spouse?

Even after David knew Bathsheba was married, he called for her and slept with her. Once he learned she was pregnant, he tried to cover it up. Let's read verses 6-13:

6 Then David sent to Joab, saying, "Send me Uriah the Hittite." So Joab sent Uriah to David. 7 When Uriah came to him, David asked concerning the welfare of Joab and the people and the state of the war. 8 Then David said to Uriah, "Go down to your house, and wash your feet." And Uriah went out of the king's house, and a present from the king was sent out after him. 9 But Uriah slept at the door of the king's house with all the servants of his lord, and did not go down to his house. 10 Now when they told David, saying, "Uriah did not go down to his house," David said to Uriah, "Have you not come from a journey? Why did you not go down to your house?" 11 Uriah said to David, "The ark and Israel and Judah are staying in temporary shelters, and my lord Joab and the servants of my lord are camping in the open field. Shall I then go to my house to eat and to drink and to lie with my wife? By your life and the life of your soul, I will not do this thing." 12 Then David said to Uriah, "Stay here today also, and tomorrow I will let you go." So Uriah remained in Jerusalem that day and the next. 13 Now David called him, and he ate and drank before him, and he made him drunk; and in the evening he went out to lie on his bed with his lord's servants, but he did not go down to his house.

12. Why was David hoping Uriah would go home and lie with (have sex with) Bathsheba?

13. What "cover up" activities can you think of that could threaten your marriage?

David's plan to get Uriah drunk so that he would go to have sex with Bathsheba didn't work, so David made a more drastic, more desperate move. Read verses 14-17:

14 Now in the morning David wrote a letter to Joab and sent it by the hand of Uriah. 15 He had written in the letter, saying, "Place Uriah in the front line of the fiercest battle and withdraw from him, so that he may be struck down and die." 16 So it was as Joab kept watch on the city, that he put Uriah at the place where he knew there were valiant men. 17 The men of the city went out and fought against Joab, and some of the people among David's servants fell; and Uriah the Hittite also died.

In your own Bible, you can read what happened next. The last sentence of that chapter sums it all up: *But the thing that David had done was evil in the sight of the Lord.*
Yikes.

Read Matthew 6:22, 23:
22 "The eye is the lamp of the body. If your eyes are healthy, your whole body will be full of light. 23 But if your eyes are unhealthy, your whole body will be full of darkness. If then

the light within you is darkness, how great is that darkness!

14. Why does it matter where you let your eyes linger?

Decisions you make about what you read, what you watch, who you notice, who you spend time with, who you listen to, and what you hide from your spouse all contribute to whether you will have a marriage that reflects God's holy romance or reflects worldly lusts.

We Time

Sexual fidelity in marriage means that your sexual energy and emotions are reserved for your spouse alone. Treat your sexual energy as a precious commodity. If you give pieces of it away to other people or other activities, you won't have what you need to give your spouse.

15. Think of a time God met a need that you and your spouse had. Describe it.

We are going to identify some categories of needs that we meet for each other.

16. Think about your emotional needs. How does your spouse meet your emotional needs?

17. Think about your physical needs. How does your spouse meet your physical needs?

18. Think about your sexual needs. How does your spouse meet your sexual needs?

19. Think about your spiritual needs. In what ways does your spouse support you in meeting your spiritual needs?

When we think of our needs, we tend to focus on the physical, sexual, or emotional needs over the spiritual. Our human minds might create a "honey-do" list of activities we wish our spouse would do. Stuff like clean the garage, mow the lawn, organize the linen closet, make a dentist appointment. We get frustrated when our spouses don't "do" the tasks we want them to "do" because we think those "needs" are most important. However, if you focus on your own and your spouse's spiritual needs, the rest will fall in line in their proper places.

Read Matthew 6:25-34 together.

25 "For this reason I say to you, do not be worried about your life, as to what you will eat or what you will drink; nor for your body, as to what you will put on. Is not life more than food, and the body more than clothing? 26 Look at the birds of the air, that they do not sow, nor reap nor gather into barns, and yet your heavenly Father feeds them. Are you not worth much more than they? 27 And who of you by being worried can add a single hour to his life? 28 And why are you worried about clothing? Observe how the lilies of the field grow; they do not toil nor do they spin, 29 yet I say to you that not even Solomon in all his glory clothed himself like one of these. 30 But if God so clothes the grass of the field, which is alive today and tomorrow is thrown into the furnace, will He not much more clothe you? You of little faith! 31 Do not worry then, saying, 'What will we eat?' or 'What will we drink?' or 'What will we wear for clothing?' 32 For the Gentiles eagerly seek all these things; for your heavenly Father knows that you need all these things. 33 But seek first His kingdom and His righteousness, and all these things will be added to you.

34 "So do not worry about tomorrow; for tomorrow will care for itself. Each day has enough trouble of its own."

20. What should your main concern be in this life?

When you focus on your spiritual needs—seeking His kingdom first—all other things will fall into line. Keep in mind though, <u>you</u> cannot meet your spouse's spiritual needs; in other words, you can't "be" God or Savior to your spouse. But you and your spouse can make the decision to put your spiritual needs first.

We don't want to belittle the fact that we have other needs aside from the spiritual. When we begin to ask God to give us an attitude of servanthood for our spouse and to show us how to meet one another's needs, we grow closer to Him and to each other in all of our need areas. For many couples, this decision helps rightly align the others.

Journal Reflection

Reflect on how God meets your needs. How does He sustain you? How would keeping focus on Him help you stay faithful in your marriage?

Closing Thoughts

How do we support our spouse's spiritual growth? Let's recap what we've learned so far.

First, we have the attitude which Jesus had: an attitude of servanthood.

Second, think back to what we learned from Paul and Silas in Lesson 2. Stay connected to the Holy Spirit through rejoicing, prayer, and thanksgiving. When you do, you are ready to respond in all situations.

Third, guard your ears. Guard your eyes. Guard your mind. Treat your sexual and emotional energy as a precious commodity. Reserve it only for your spouse. If there are things you need to stop doing, make that decision today.

Our next focus will be on a little five-letter word with big power: trust.

Lesson 4
The Decision to Trust

Lesson Introduction

There more than 60,000 books on Amazon with the word "trust" in the title. Many of these fall into the Self-Help genre and are themed around building trust in various situations we find ourselves in: *Build Trust at Work, Build Trust in Your Marriage, Build Trusting Relationships*, and the like. Humans have trust issues, don't we?

When one person in a marriage does not trust another, the fracture in the relationship will only grow bigger if the trust is not addressed. Marital trust can be broken in different ways, but it almost always begins with dishonesty.

Because trust is difficult to compartmentalize, once trust is broken in one area, all others are affected. If a wife is dishonest with finances, for example, the mistrust the husband has will seep into other areas where he feels he can't take her at her word. When broken trust happens when it comes to fidelity, some couples never recover.

We don't want that to be the case for our marriages, though, do we? In this week's lesson we are going to address the concept of trust and take a biblical look at how we should frame trust to have a rightful place in our lives.

Trust and Expectations

Think of the process of using a recipe to make a dessert. You begin with a specific list of ingredients. You complete the instructions in the correct order, using the correct techniques for combining the ingredients. When it is done correctly, voilà! You have a perfect finished product.

You trust that following the steps will produce the desired outcome. You know what to expect at the end because the title of the dessert (and sometimes even a picture!) is given. Recipes allow us to cook with reliability. You wouldn't follow a recipe for black forest cake and expect to have a lemon pie at the end. That makes no sense! You trust the black forest cake recipe to produce a black forest cake.

When we say that we "trust" someone, what we often mean is that we have come to expect certain things from them. We treat them like a recipe. We expect them to follow certain steps and give a certain result. We've placed an expectation on them, and if they don't come through, we are frustrated. If they said they would do something and they don't, we might get angry. If the expectation is something unspoken, and we feel they've let us down, we can harbor resentment. If there has been a betrayal, the pain in your heart can be overwhelming.

At any level, failed expectations are at the root of any "trust" problem. The intensity of the disappointment or hurt is relational to how close you are to the person who has failed you.

In a marriage relationship, failed expectations have the highest propensity for hurt. This relationship is to be your closest! Under God's protective wings, the friendship between you and your spouse should be the safest place. When it isn't, things aren't as they should be.

Measures of Trust

If you are familiar with Star Wars, you may be familiar with this line by Yoda, the Jedi Master: "Do or do not, there is no try." We'd like to suggest that when it comes to trust, a parallel all-or-nothing concept applies. You trust or you do not trust. There is no in-between. The nature of the word "trust" leaves no room for doubt. The question becomes: What do you trust in?

Think of it this way, you probably trust your kids with

some things, but not others. It isn't that you don't trust them at all, but you are careful what you trust them with. You might trust a coworker with certain aspects of a project, but not others. You are aware of where you can put your expectations based on a person's past behavior.

When a heart has been hurt because a spouse has failed in a promise or expectation, rebuilding trust must happen for the marriage to survive, and it will take work on the part of both spouses.

The spouse who has been hurt must begin to give the other person opportunities to build trust again, little by little. The spouse who has done the wrong must accept the fact that he or she must show to be faithful in the small things, until the trust can be built in the bigger things. It is a process of give and take, vulnerability and reliability. The spouse who has been hurt has to be willing to be vulnerable again. The spouse who broke trust must come through as reliable.

And friends, none of it is possible without God. He has much to teach us about trust and being trustworthy. Let's study some of those Scriptures now.

The Spicy Meatball...
The most important ingredient for a healthy marriage is complete trust that God's way is the best way to do things.

1. How does the above statement make you feel? Do you agree?

Me Time

2. Look up the Bible verses in the chart below. Each has a message for us regarding trust. What is the "trust instruction" given in each verse?

Bible Verses	Trust Instruction
Proverbs 3:5	
Psalm 40:4	
Psalm 56:3,4	
Jeremiah 17:5	
Jeremiah 17:7	

Trust is an abstract concept. That means, trust is not something you can experience with your five senses; it is an intangible feeling or belief that comes from within.

To make the concept of trust come alive for us, we are going to look at two Hebrew words that express similar connotations as our word trust. We believe this will make the Old Testament verses more vivid for you, as the Hebrew language is concrete-oriented. Hebrew words are often associated with one or more of the five senses (sight, touch, sound, smell, taste), giving depth in meaning or nuances that aid us in interpreting the writer's message.

Batach

The first word we will study is the word **batach.** This word is closely linked to **betach** (pronounced beh'takh), which means "to have security in" or "a place of refuge."[11]

This word is made up of three Hebrew letters:
bet / tet / chet
- The "bet" part of this word presents the picture of a tent or home.
- The "tet" part of this word paints the picture of being wrapped around or coiled around something.
- The "chet" part of this word indicates a fence or wall.

With these word pictures in mind, read the following verses:
*For our heart rejoices in Him, Because we **trust** in His holy name.* (Psalm 33:21)

*He **trusted** in the Lord, the God of Israel; so that after him there was none like him among all the kings of Judah, nor among those who were before him.* (2 Kings 18:5)

*But I have **trusted** in Your lovingkindness; My heart shall rejoice in Your salvation.* (Psalm 13:5)

3. How does the Hebrew definition add meaning to these verses for you?

4. According to these verses, what qualities of God's should be your safe place of refuge?

Aman

Aman (pronounced aw-man') means to confirm or support something.[12] This can indicate the kind of support that a doorpost or pillar provides, but most frequently in Scripture it is a confirmation of belief or trust in something. It is surety, a foundation upon which you can stand firm.

What really adds depth to verses which include **aman** in the Hebrew language is that aman has the same root as the word **amen**. Christians use "amen" to declare agreement with whatever has been said, prayed, or preached when we want to underscore our confirmation of it.

Did you know? Moses was the first person to call for people to declare their trust and confidence in a message by declaring "amen!" Read these verses from Deuteronomy 27:

15 'Cursed is the man who makes an idol or a molten image, an abomination to the Lord, the work of the hands of the craftsman, and sets it up in secret.' And all the people shall answer and say, 'Amen.'

16 'Cursed is he who dishonors his father or mother.' And all the people shall say, 'Amen.'

17 'Cursed is he who moves his neighbor's boundary mark.' And all the people shall say, 'Amen.'

18 'Cursed is he who misleads a blind person on the road.' And all the people shall say, 'Amen.'

19 'Cursed is he who distorts the justice due an alien, orphan, and widow.' And all the people shall say, 'Amen.'

20 'Cursed is he who lies with his father's wife, because he has uncovered his father's skirt.' And all the people shall say, 'Amen.'

21 'Cursed is he who lies with any animal.' And all the people shall say, 'Amen.'

22 'Cursed is he who lies with his sister, the daughter of his father or of his mother.' And all the people shall say, 'Amen.'

23 'Cursed is he who lies with his mother-in-law.' And all the people shall say, 'Amen.'

24 'Cursed is he who strikes his neighbor in secret.' And all the people shall say, 'Amen.'

25 'Cursed is he who accepts a bribe to strike down an innocent person.' And all the people shall say, 'Amen.'

26 'Cursed is he who does not confirm the words of this law by doing them.' And all the people shall say, 'Amen.'

Moses leaves it clear that idol worship, dishonesty, sexual sin, and disobedience will be punished. But what is interesting is that in delivering this part of his message, he instructs that all the people confirm the rule, showing trust in the commands, giving their support and agreement with it by declaring, "Amen."

When you say, "amen," you can picture that you are placing trust in what has been said. You are declaring that it is a foundation to depend on.

5. How does knowing that the root of the word "amen" involves a firm foundation of trust impact how you think about its use?

6. Think about the qualities of God that you personally cling to, stand firm on, believe deeply as truth. What do you place your trust in God for?

7. Refer back to the "Trust Instructions" you identified on page 52. What does the Bible say about trusting in man?

8. What does "trusting in man" look like in your life? What areas do you need to shift trust from man to God?

9. What is your knee-jerk reaction when your spouse does something outside of your expectations?

When we get angry with our spouse for not meeting our expectations or breaking our trust, it is often because:
- Our expectations are worldly-focused
- We have not communicated what we expect
- Our expectations are not realistic

What we want you to see is that the trust we are to place in God is not the same trust we place in our spouse (or any worldly thing).

Trusting God means you place a deep belief in Him for your refuge, your firm foundation, security, protection, and truth. Your marriage should indeed be a place of refuge, security, protection, and truth, but ONLY because it has God at the center. If your refuge is in the worldly things that people bring into a marriage (like finances, sex, or to-do lists), you will inevitably be disappointed. Why? We are not to place our trust in those man-made things. The opposite of trusting God is not "doubting God," it is trusting man.

10. We started this lesson's study talking about expectations we place on other people, and specifically our spouse. Ask God to reveal any areas where you have placed expectations on your spouse that are "you-based" rather than "God-based." List anything that comes to mind.

We Time

The world showers us with lies about marriage. You may see other couples who appear to have it all together, who say and do the right things, and who make you feel that your marriage is inferior. The world will also say that if your marriage isn't what you expect it to be, then it is OK to leave your marriage and find another. It will instruct that if you have feelings of unhappiness, then you should find someone who makes you happy; if you are unsatisfied, you deserve to be satisfied. The world will tell you that your marriage is all about you.

Friends, these worldly lies will impact the trust you place in your spouse. The world's expectations will become those you carry. You must avoid the temptation to let the expectations on your marriage be worldly.

Read together 1 John 4:

1 Beloved, do not believe every spirit, but test the spirits to see whether they are from God, because many false prophets have gone out into the world. 2 By this you know the Spirit of God: every spirit that confesses that Jesus Christ has come in the flesh is from God; 3 and every spirit that does not confess Jesus is not from God; this is the spirit of the antichrist, of which you have heard that it is coming, and now it is already in the world. 4 You are from God, little children, and have overcome them; because greater is He who is in you than he who is in the world. 5 They are from the world; therefore they speak as from the world, and the world listens to them. 6 We are from God; he who knows God listens to us; he who is not from God does not listen to us. By this we know the spirit of truth and the spirit of error.

God Is Love
7 Beloved, let us love one another, for love is from God; and everyone who loves is born of God and knows God. 8 The one who does not love does not know God, for God is love. 9 By this the love of God was manifested in us, that God has sent His only begotten Son into the world so that we might live through Him. 10 In this is love, not that we loved God, but that He loved us and sent His Son to be the propitiation for our sins. 11 Beloved, if God so loved us, we also ought to love one another. 12 No one has seen God at any time; if we love one

another, God abides in us, and His love is perfected in us. 13 By this we know that we abide in Him and He in us, because He has given us of His Spirit. 14 We have seen and testify that the Father has sent the Son to be the Savior of the world.

15 Whoever confesses that Jesus is the Son of God, God abides in him, and he in God. 16 We have come to know and have believed the love which God has for us. God is love, and the one who abides in love abides in God, and God abides in him. 17 By this, love is perfected with us, so that we may have confidence in the day of judgment; because as He is, so also are we in this world. 18 There is no fear in love; but perfect love casts out fear, because fear involves punishment, and the one who fears is not perfected in love. 19 We love, because He first loved us. 20 If someone says, "I love God," and hates his brother, he is a liar; for the one who does not love his brother whom he has seen, cannot love God whom he has not seen. 21 And this commandment we have from Him, that the one who loves God should love his brother also.

11. Highlight or circle every mention of the word **world** in verses 1-6. What do these verses tell you about the **world**?

12. Read verses 7-14. How do we know that God loves us?

13. What does verse 14 have to say about "the world"?

14. Are there areas of your marriage that you are afraid to entrust completely to God? List them below. Talk about them with your spouse.

15. Are there areas of your marriage where miscommunication, past mistakes, or worldly definitions of marriage have caused a fracture in trust? Without reliving the experience, acknowledge it below. Are you afraid to allow space for that trust to be strengthened?

16. Reread verses 16-18. What do these verses have to say about the relationship between God's love and fear?

17. When you feel afraid to trust, what can you do
individually and as a couple to cast out the fear?

18. Together with your spouse, make a list of God-honoring
expectations you can commit to in your marriage.

Journal Reflection

What worldly things do you allow to influence the
expectations you place on your spouse? This can
come in the form of entertainment, books, family, friends,
music, social media. Reflect on anything you are letting in
which should not have a voice in your expectations.

Closing Thoughts

The abstract feeling of trust touches every part of our
lives. We trust our cars to run properly, our employers to
pay us on time, our coffee to work its morning magic, our
doctors to help us when we're sick... and when it comes to

marriage, we trust our spouse to meet our needs. We can always get a new car, find a new job, or get a new doctor, but what do we do when a spouse has let us down?

The first recognition is that trust in the Lord is a deep belief in God alone for our refuge, our strength, our security, our strong tower. We are not to place that kind of foundational trust in anything in the world. Our marriages reflect these qualities only when God is at the center.

"Trusting" things in this world really is just a management of our expectations. If the expectations we place on our spouse come from a worldly point of view, we will always be let down. We must communicate clearly, keep a godly perspective, and ensure realistic expectations. When trust has been broken, both must recognize there is a give and take of vulnerability and reliability to rebuild and restore the relationship.

God tells us to look to His love when we feel fear. This includes when we are afraid to trust. Will you look to Him in all things and trust that His way is the best way to proceed?

Trusting God can involve:
- o Obeying the straightforward commands of the Bible
- o Praying in all situations
- o Seeking what the Bible instructs when you need clarity on a matter
- o Gaining counsel from a godly source
- o Commitment to follow through, even if things are hard

There is another component to maintaining a marriage that reflects God's holy romance: forgiveness. We will look at the decision to forgive in our next lesson.

Lesson 5
The Decision to Forgive

Lesson Introduction

Our daily lives are flooded with choices when it comes to sports, politics, medical news, and entertainment. Are you conservative or liberal? Will you root for the favorite or the underdog? Are you pro-vaxx or anti-vaxx? It seems like humans are wired to pick sides, and we're always ready to give our opinions. A favorite road trip game in our van is "Would You Rather?" in which players choose between two options and explain the reasons behind their choice.

Many people <u>don't</u>, however, like to openly pick sides when it comes to matters of faith. We keep our opinions to ourselves. But the fact remains that when it comes to your faith, you have only one of two options: you are either saved, or you are not. There is no in-between. You can't be a little bit of a Christian. You are either Team God or Team Satan.

That doesn't sit well with many because no common-sense thinking person wants to think they are sided with the devil. But Scripture makes it very clear: you can't be a child of God and a child of the world. You are grafted into God's family tree when you put your trust in Jesus for salvation and forgiveness of your sins and commit to giving Him Lordship over your life. When you are saved, you want to do things His way, not your way.

We open with these statements because what we will study this week—forgiveness—is a behavior that believers in Christ are called to demonstrate. It is not optional! And if we seek for our marriages to reflect Christ's love for His church, then we must put a magnifying glass to our attitudes towards forgiveness and make changes where the Holy Spirit shows us change must be made.

Forgiveness Your Way

There is a quote that reads: "Unforgiveness is like drinking poison and waiting for the other person to die." This quote has been attributed to several authors and the word unforgiveness is sometimes replaced with "resentment" or "harboring bitterness." The gist of the sentiment is when you hold on to those feelings, you aren't hurting the other person as much as you are hurting yourself. Feelings of unforgiveness, bitterness, and resentment toward another are like poison to your soul.

We wouldn't intentionally drink poison, now would we? Of course not! So in our humanness, we try to justify our unforgiveness. Have you ever thought if you forgive someone, it is like giving permission for the wrong that has been done? Or perhaps if you forgive too quickly, you are letting someone off the hook? Have you made someone wait a certain amount of time before you let them back into your good graces? Do you wait until someone actually says that they are sorry before you'll forgive them?

People put different parameters on the things they will and won't forgive. "I could never forgive him if..." "I'll never forgive her for..." "I won't forgive him unless he..."

There are a lot of people walking around with the poison of unforgiveness sloshing around their gullets. As a child of God, hear us when we say, "It is not to be this way with you!" (Matthew 20:26)

The decision to forgive is one of the most powerful you can make as a Christian. Adopting an attitude of forgiveness in your marriage will transform it completely.

The Spicy Meatball...
If you choose not to forgive others in your heart,
Jesus will not forgive you.

1. How does the above statement make you feel?

Me Time

This week's Spicy Meatball is pretty spicy, so to begin our study, we want to explore two of the Scriptures that support it.

Read Matthew 18:21-35:

21 Then Peter came and said to Him, "Lord, how often shall my brother sin against me and I forgive him? Up to seven times?" 22 Jesus said to him, "I do not say to you, up to seven times, but up to seventy times seven.

23 For this reason the kingdom of heaven may be compared to a king who wished to settle accounts with his slaves. 24 When he had begun to settle them, one who owed him ten thousand talents was brought to him. 25 But since he did not have the means to repay, his lord commanded him to be sold, along with his wife and children and all that he had, and repayment to be made.

26 So the slave fell to the ground and prostrated himself before him, saying, 'Have patience with me and I will repay you everything.' 27 And the lord of that slave felt compassion and released him and forgave him the debt.

28 But that slave went out and found one of his fellow slaves who owed him a hundred denarii; and he seized him and began to choke him, saying, 'Pay back what you owe.' 29 So his fellow slave fell to the ground and began to plead with him, saying, 'Have patience with me and I will repay you.' 30 But he was unwilling and went and threw him in prison until he should pay back what was owed.

31 So when his fellow slaves saw what had happened, they were deeply grieved and came and reported to their lord all that had happened.

32 Then summoning him, his lord said to him, 'You wicked slave, I forgave you all that debt because you pleaded with me. 33 Should you not also have had mercy on your fellow slave, in the same way that I had mercy on you?' 34 And his lord, moved with anger, handed him over to the torturers until he should repay all that was owed him.

35 My heavenly Father will also do the same to you, if each of you does not forgive his brother from your heart."

2. What was Peter's question in verse 21?

3. Jesus responds with a parable about a king and a slave, each presented with an opportunity to forgive another. The king and the slave demonstrate very different reactions when asked for forgiveness. Make note of how each responds:

KING (v.27)	SLAVE (v.30)

4. How do we know that the lesson in this parable is also a lesson for us? (see verses 23, 35)

5. What was the outcome for the unforgiving slave?

Read Mark 11:25,26:

25 Whenever you stand praying, forgive, if you have anything against anyone, so that your Father who is in heaven will also forgive you your transgressions. 26 [But if you do not forgive, neither will your Father who is in heaven forgive your transgressions."]

6. Who and what does Jesus say we should forgive?

7. Highlight in verse 25 WHY we should forgive.

8. What do these two passages of Scripture reveal about forgiveness?

If Jesus instructs us to forgive others, why is it so difficult? Often, we hesitate to forgive, even when it is our spouse, because we feel like if we do, we are letting the other person get away with something. Friend, we hope you notice that the forgiveness isn't for them, Jesus says it is for YOU!

Family hurts can be some of the most difficult to forgive. If there were ever someone who would have earned the "right" to harbor resentment, it would have been Joseph in the Old Testament. You can read about it beginning in Genesis 37. To summarize: Joseph's brothers were wildly jealous of him. They plotted his death against him and sold him into slavery. A mix-up, in which Potiphar's wife tried to seduce him and he rejected her, landed him in prison. He was released after two years, when Pharaoh saw that Joseph had wisdom (given to him from God). Joseph's God-given visions helped save the Egyptians from the famine which ravaged Egypt. It was a very different life from what young Joseph envisioned for himself.

Many years later, those same brothers who sold Joseph away came to Egypt seeking help. The famine was on, and they were starving. They would die without the food that Joseph controlled. They didn't know it was their brother Joseph who held their fate in his hands. Look what Joseph did:

Read Genesis 45:10-15:

10 You shall live in the land of Goshen, and you shall be near me, you and your children and your children's children and your flocks and your herds and all that you have. 11 There I will also provide for you, for there are still five years of famine to come, and you and your household and all that you have would be impoverished.'" 12 Behold, your eyes see, and the eyes of my brother Benjamin see, that it is my mouth which is speaking to you. 13 Now you must tell my father of all my splendor in Egypt, and all that you have seen; and you must hurry and bring my father down here." 14 Then he fell on his brother Benjamin's neck and wept, and Benjamin wept on his neck. 15 He kissed all his brothers and wept on them, and afterward his brothers talked with him.

8. Highlight Joseph's words in verse 11 and his actions in verse 15. What impact did Joseph's forgiveness have on the brothers? How might it have impacted them spiritually?

Lewis B. Smedes wrote, "To forgive is to set a prisoner free and discover that the prisoner was you."[13]

This study is focused on strengthening your marriage, but unforgiveness of anyone in your life must be addressed because it **will** impact your marriage. Just as it is difficult to compartmentalize trust, it is impossible to hold bitter, resentful feelings in one area of your life and not have it spill into others. When you hold onto hurt, you will inevitably hurt someone else. Hurting people tend to hurt other people.

9. Who do you need to forgive, in order for your own heart to be set free?

We Time

The most quoted Scripture at weddings are the verses found in 1 Corinthians 13. Even nonbelievers quote from this passage when exchanging wedding vows. We will begin our We Time by reading it together:

1 If I speak with the tongues of men and of angels, but do not have love, I have become a noisy gong or a clanging cymbal. 2 If I have the gift of prophecy, and know all mysteries and all knowledge; and if I have all faith, so as to remove mountains, but do not have love, I am nothing. 3 And if I give all my possessions to feed the poor, and if I surrender my body to be burned, but do not have love, it profits me nothing.

4 Love is patient, love is kind and is not jealous; love does not brag and is not arrogant, 5 does not act unbecomingly; it does not seek its own, is not provoked, does not take into account a wrong suffered, 6 does not rejoice in unrighteousness, but rejoices with the truth; 7 bears all things, believes all things, hopes all things, endures all things.

8 Love never fails; but if there are gifts of prophecy, they will be done away; if there are tongues, they will cease; if there is knowledge, it will be done away. 9 For we know in part and we prophesy in part; 10 but when the perfect comes, the partial will be done away. 11 When I was a child, I used to speak like a child, think like a child, reason like a child; when I became a man, I did away with childish things. 12 For now we see in a mirror dimly, but then face to face; now I know in part, but then I will know fully just as I also have been fully known. 13 But now faith, hope, love, abide these three; but the greatest of these is love.

These verses are quoted at weddings because they reflect the kind of love we want to be seen in our marriage.

Paul wasn't thinking of wedding verses though when he wrote this. He was explaining how believers are to act if we are showing Christ's love.

   We are to show Christ's love to everyone, and that certainly includes our spouses.

10. Let's rewrite verses 4-7, substituting your name for the word "love."

_____ is patient

_____ is kind

_____ is not jealous

_____ does not brag and is not arrogant

_____ does not act unbecomingly

_____ does not seek his/her own

_____ is not provoked

_____ does not take into account a wrong suffered

_____ does not rejoice in unrighteousness

_____ rejoices with the truth

_____ bears all things

_____ believes all things

_____ hopes all things

_____ endures all things

Can you write your name on the lines and feel good about the truth of it? These verses provide a shockingly clear definition of Christ's love in action.

You and your spouse can make the decision to forgive any wrongs past, present, and future so that bitterness and resentment have no hold on your hearts. It is the thing Christ commands us to do. It might not be easy, but we have a way through.

Read these verses from Matthew 14:

22 Immediately He made the disciples get into the boat and go ahead of Him to the other side, while He sent the crowds away. 23 After He had sent the crowds away, He went up on the mountain by Himself to pray; and when it was evening, He was there alone. 24 But the boat was already a long distance from the land, battered by the waves; for the wind was contrary. 25 And in the fourth watch of the night He came to them, walking on the sea. 26 When the disciples saw Him walking on the sea, they were terrified, and said, "It is a ghost!" And they cried out in fear. 27 But immediately Jesus spoke to them, saying, "Take courage, it is I; do not be afraid."

28 Peter said to Him, "Lord, if it is You, command me to come to You on the water." 29 And He said, "Come!" And Peter got out of the boat, and walked on the water and came toward Jesus. 30 But seeing the wind, he became frightened, and beginning to sink, he cried out, "Lord, save me!" 31 Immediately Jesus stretched out His hand and took hold of him, and said to him, "You of little faith, why did you doubt?" 32 When they got into the boat, the wind stopped. 33 And those who were in the boat worshiped Him, saying, "You are certainly God's Son!"

11. Take note of the weather. The wind caused the boat to be battered by the waves, causing terror and fear in the disciples. So much so, that they forgot that Jesus was nearby. What storms of life threaten to make you and your spouse forget that Jesus is nearby? What "batters your boat"?

Peter knew that the answer to their problem was to make it to Jesus. That is our answer, too, when we are sinking in the waves of emotions that life brings. The good news is that we can learn from Peter's actions and apply them to our situations. There are three actions Peter took.

1. Look for Jesus

Jesus was there when the storms threatened to overtake them. They felt the danger, but were never going to be overtaken by those waves. In your situations, even when it feels like you will be overtaken by emotions or situational difficulties, you will not. Jesus is there, and your peace begins when you look for Him.

Read Isaiah 43:1-3
"Do not fear, for I have redeemed you;
I have called you by name; you are Mine!
2 "When you pass through the waters, I will be with you;
And through the rivers, they will not overflow you.
When you walk through the fire, you will not be scorched,
Nor will the flame burn you.
3 "For I am the Lord your God,
The Holy One of Israel, your Savior;

12. When you are in a difficult situation, do you and your spouse make it a practice to look for Jesus? If so, how? If not, what can you do differently?

2. Connect with Jesus

Peter saw Jesus approaching. He knew he needed to connect with Him. He felt the fear, but Peter got out of the boat anyway! This is an incredible act of faith. He knew that battered boat wasn't the thing that would save him from the storm. He knew he had to put his feelings aside in order to survive. He knew it was Jesus alone who could help. He had to get past the boat to get to Jesus.

13. What stands in the way of your connection with Jesus when emotional turbulence and feelings like unforgiveness threaten your marriage? Is it pride? Fear? Control issues?

14. What do you need to do to "get out of the boat" in those moments to connect with Jesus?

3. Trust Jesus
As Peter started towards his Lord, he took his eyes off of Jesus just for a moment and gave his focus to the waves, wind, and storm around them. And when he did, Peter started to sink. But he called out, "Lord save me!"

15. Read Matthew 14:31. How did Jesus respond to Peter's cry for help?

16. How does the real-life story of Peter in Matthew 14 support the promise written by Isaiah in Isaiah 43?

17. Discuss as a couple your thoughts on these promises. What do you find encouraging? How can you support each other when things are stormy?

Can you imagine the expressions on the apostles' faces when Peter got out of that boat? No doubt they wanted to save their friend when he started to sink. Maybe John was getting a rope ready to toss to Peter. But Peter put the other voices aside. He didn't look to his friends to save him. (Even though they were pretty great guys!) He didn't look at any worldly thing. He looked to Jesus.

Journal Reflection

How is unforgiveness like a storm? In what situations might you be tempted to hold on to resentment? What will you do to be saved from it?

Closing Thoughts

We often think of the difficulties of life being situational like a loss of a job, financial hardship, health problems. And these things do create storms around and within us. We want you to see, though, that holding on to past hurts will also cause turbulence in your heart that can feel like the wind battering your boat. Unforgiveness raging inside of a person will run like poison throughout your soul. We must forgive, for our own sakes!

Jesus is right there, ready to help you when you need it. When you are tempted to act in a way that is outside of God's definitions of love, look for Him, connect with Him, trust Him.

We know forgiveness is tough, but when you understand the magnitude of your own forgiveness and have a clear sense of purpose for your own life, it becomes increasingly easier. In our next lesson we will explore the decision to surrender.

Lesson 6
The Decision to Surrender

Lesson Introduction

Let's take a moment to recap what we have covered in our lessons thus far:

Lesson 1 - An attitude of **servanthood** towards your spouse is a key characteristic of a marriage that reflects the love of Christ.

Lesson 2 - Spouses should **pray** together regularly and in all things. Change begins with prayer.

Lesson 3 - **Faithfulness** in marriage can be safeguarded by being ruthlessly protective of your emotional and sexual energy. Do not allow worldly voices to dictate how your marriage should be.

Lesson 4 - Our ultimate **trust** is to be in God alone. His promises are our refuge and stronghold. Our marriages reflect this trust only when God is at the center.

Lesson 5 - **Forgiveness** is not optional in the life of a believer. Loving each other God's way includes forgiving all wrongs. Harboring unforgiveness will destroy us from the inside.

Put into practice, these principles will transform your marriage. They are based on God's way of showing love, and God's love is a transforming love. With two lessons to go in our study, we are going to zero in more closely on making the decision to surrender to our own selfishness so that we can make the decision to love our spouses completely.

Surrender

In the 1800s, author Edgar Allen Poe wrote, "Years of love have been forgot in the hatred of a minute."[14]

How many marriages have been severed in the heat of the moment, with years of love being forgotten for want of the pleasure of being right in the minute? Words spoken aloud cannot be retrieved. We may deeply regret them, but we can never take them back.

The heat of the moment is a dangerous place to be. Something has happened, and we are unexpectedly faced with having to respond. Human emotions surface very quickly. Anger, shock, hurt, fear, disappointment, disgust... your past experiences and attitudes will dictate what bubbles up when you feel your spouse has failed you. And more often than not, your response to bubbling emotions puts you on the defense. You dig your heels in to fight. Whatever love has been built up blows away in the wind. You step out of your spouse's corner and put on the boxing gloves.

Nothing good happens when both spouses are wearing boxing gloves.

But there is good news.

Once you accept Christ, you are given the gift of the Holy Spirit. He takes up residence inside of you, and one of His jobs is to teach and guide you in God's wisdom and love. When something happens that brings out negative or painful human emotions, before you act or speak, you can ask the Holy Spirit to guide your response. You can surrender your response to Jesus. The more you practice surrendering in difficult moments, the stronger you will become at hearing the voice of the Lord guiding you into right responses. The gap between the inciting incident and your actions will grow wider, and in the gap, you will find the response that will show your spouse God's love.

This is the first act of surrender to embrace. Surrendering to the truth that in all situations, God's response is the best course of action. From the world's perspective, surrender is a bad thing. Surrender indicates defeat. From a biblical perspective, it is only when we surrender that we are victorious. Does that seem like a contradiction? In 1 Corinthians 1:18,19 Paul writes, *"For the word of the cross is foolishness to those who are perishing, but to us who are being saved it is the power of God. For it is written, 'I will destroy the wisdom of the wise, And the cleverness of the clever I will set aside.'"*

Those who do not believe will not understand how surrender can bring victory. But you, believer, have the power of the Holy Spirit in you to guide you in all wisdom. Pause right now and pray. Ask the Holy Spirit to give you clarity and right understanding of what a follower of Christ is required to surrender in our own spiritual lives and in our marriages.

The Spicy Meatball...
There will be times when God's response to a situation will NOT be the thing you want to surrender to.

1. How do you feel about the above statement?

Me Time

2. Think about a time when you knew the right thing to do, but you chose not to do it. How did you feel? Were there consequences?

Read Isaiah 30:18-21
18 Therefore the Lord longs to be gracious to you,
And therefore He waits on high to have compassion on you.
For the Lord is a God of justice;
How blessed are all those who long for Him.

19 O people in Zion, inhabitant in Jerusalem, you will weep no longer. He will surely be gracious to you at the sound of your cry; when He hears it, He will answer you. 20 Although the Lord has given you bread of privation and water of oppression, He, your Teacher will no longer hide Himself, but your eyes will behold your Teacher. 21 Your ears will hear a word behind you, "This is the way, walk in it," whenever you turn to the right or to the left.

3. The last line of verse 18 tells us who these verses are for: those who long for Him. Then there is a promise given. What is that promise?

Read Proverbs 3:5-8
5 Trust in the Lord with all your heart
And do not lean on your own understanding.
6 In all your ways acknowledge Him,
And He will make your paths straight.
7 Do not be wise in your own eyes;
Fear the Lord and turn away from evil.
8 It will be healing to your body
And refreshment to your bones.

4. What do these verses teach about the importance of surrendering your reactions and responses to the Lord?

5. How do these verses relate to marriage?

6. When, in marriage, is it most difficult to surrender your responses to the Lord?

7. Why is it important that we surrender how we respond to the Lord?

Biblically, we can understand that God wants us to listen for His voice to guide us through our day. We can see the value in responding to situations, especially difficult ones, God's way instead of man's way. But what gets in the way of our loving responses?

Read James 4:1-7:
1 What is the source of quarrels and conflicts among you? Is not the source your pleasures that wage war in your members? 2 You lust and do not have; so you commit murder. You are envious and cannot obtain; so you fight and quarrel. You do not have because you do not ask. 3 You ask and do not receive, because you ask with wrong motives, so that you may spend it on your pleasures. 4 You adulteresses, do you not know that friendship with the world is hostility toward God? Therefore whoever wishes to be a friend of the world makes himself an enemy of God. 5 Or do you think that the Scripture speaks to no purpose: "He jealously desires the Spirit which He has made to dwell in us"? 6 But He gives a greater grace. Therefore it says, "God is opposed to the proud, but gives grace to the humble." 7 Submit therefore to God. Resist the devil and he will flee from you.

8. These verses provide reasons for the conflict among us. What are they?

9. What is the solution to our conflict? It is given in verse 7.

Salvation doesn't happen unless you surrender your life to God. The act of declaring His sovereignty and accepting the gift of salvation through Jesus Christ **is** surrender. You confess your sins and have a change of heart about your sinful ways, surrendering them to God. You desire to be more like Christ, surrendering your desire to be like the world. Salvation and surrender go hand in hand.

The surrender you made at your salvation is only the beginning of your new life. You are a new creation (2 Corinthians 5:17), but old habits can persist. The devil will use those old habits to try and hold you back from living in the victory of your salvation. This is why the spiritual practices we've talked about are so important. They keep you and your spouse positioned for growth in your faith.

10. Think back to the day you accepted Christ. What brought you to the place of surrender?

11. What does surrender look like in a marriage relationship? (We are going to revisit this question in our We Time)

We fight surrendering to God's ways when it comes to matters related to marriage when we feel like surrendering will be a sign of weakness or when our pride is involved. But our surrender pales in comparison to the surrender that Jesus demonstrated to the Father. Read and notice how these verses work together.

Read John 6:38, 39:
38 For I have come down from heaven, not to do My own will, but the will of Him who sent Me. 39 This is the will of Him who sent Me, that of all that He has given Me I lose nothing, but raise it up on the last day.

Read Matthew 26:38, 39:
38 Then He said to them, "My soul is deeply grieved, to the point of death; remain here and keep watch with Me."

39 And He went a little beyond them, and fell on His face and prayed, saying, "My Father, if it is possible, let this cup pass from Me; yet not as I will, but as You will."

The cup that Jesus speaks of in Matthew 26:39 is the same cup He referred to in Lesson 1, when we studied Mark 10:39. Here is how that "cup" plays out, as found in Matthew 27:28-50:

28 They stripped Him and put a scarlet robe on Him. 29 And after twisting together a crown of thorns, they put it on His head, and a reed in His right hand; and they knelt down before Him and mocked Him, saying, "Hail, King of the Jews!" 30 They spat on Him, and took the reed and began to beat Him on the head. 31 After they had mocked Him, they took the scarlet robe off Him and put His own garments back on Him, and led Him away to crucify Him.

32 As they were coming out, they found a man of Cyrene named Simon, whom they pressed into service to bear His cross.

The Crucifixion
33 And when they came to a place called Golgotha, which means Place of a Skull, 34 they gave Him wine to drink mixed with gall; and after tasting it, He was unwilling to drink.

35 And when they had crucified Him, they divided up His garments among themselves by casting lots. 36 And sitting down, they began to keep watch over Him there. 37 And above His head they put up the charge against Him which read, "THIS IS JESUS THE KING OF THE JEWS."

38 At that time two robbers were crucified with Him, one on the right and one on the left. 39 And those passing by were hurling abuse at Him, wagging their heads 40 and saying, "You who are going to destroy the temple and rebuild it in three days, save Yourself! If You are the Son of God, come down from the cross." 41 In the same way the chief priests also, along with the scribes and elders, were mocking Him and saying, 42 "He saved others; He cannot save Himself. He is the King of Israel; let Him now come down from the cross, and we will believe in Him. 43 He trusts in God; let God rescue Him now, if He delights in Him; for He said, 'I am the Son of God.'" 44 The robbers who had been crucified with Him were also insulting Him with the same words.

45 Now from the sixth hour darkness fell upon all the land until the ninth hour. 46 About the ninth hour Jesus cried out with a loud voice, saying, "Eli, Eli, lama sabachthani?" that is, "My God, My God, why have You forsaken Me?" 47 And some of those who were standing there, when they heard it, began saying, "This man is calling for Elijah." 48 Immediately one of them ran, and taking a sponge, he filled it with sour wine and put it on a reed, and gave Him a drink. 49 But the rest of them said, "Let us see whether Elijah will come to save Him." 50 And Jesus cried out again with a loud voice, and yielded up His spirit.

Luke 23:46 records the moment of Jesus's death this way:
46 And Jesus, crying out with a loud voice, said, "Father, into Your hands I commit My spirit." Having said this, He breathed His last.

When we truly understand what Jesus surrendered for our sakes, we should see any earthly surrendering we are called to do as a privilege. That doesn't mean it is easy, but the Jesus who surrendered His life for you empowers you through His Spirit to help you. You aren't surrendering on your own.

12. What comfort does it bring to know that when you are called to surrender by demonstrating God's love in a difficult situation, you have the power of Christ to help you?

We Time

Submission and servanthood are two sides of the same coin. The more you submit to God, the easier it will be to carry an attitude of servanthood for your spouse. Likewise, when you make the choice to serve, you'll find yourself growing stronger in your faith.

On the very night that Jesus was going to be handed over to crucifixion, He demonstrated an incredible act of servanthood.

Read together John 13:1-5:
1 Now before the Feast of the Passover, Jesus knowing that His hour had come that He would depart out of this world to the Father, having loved His own who were in the world, He loved them to the end. 2 During supper, the devil having already put into the heart of Judas Iscariot, the son of Simon, to betray Him, 3 Jesus, knowing that the Father had given all things into His hands, and that He had come forth from God and was going back to God, 4 got up from supper, and laid aside His garments; and taking a towel, He girded Himself.
5 Then He poured water into the basin, and began to wash the disciples' feet and to wipe them with the towel with which He was girded.

There are so many important lessons in these verses!

13. According to these verses, what did Jesus "know"?

Read John 13:21-27:
21 When Jesus had said this, He became troubled in spirit, and testified and said, "Truly, truly, I say to you, that one of you will betray Me." 22 The disciples began looking at one another, at a loss to know of which one He was speaking. 23 There was reclining on Jesus' bosom one of His disciples, whom Jesus loved. 24 So Simon Peter gestured to him, and said to him, "Tell us who it is of whom He is speaking." 25 He, leaning back thus on Jesus' bosom, said to Him, "Lord, who is it?" 26 Jesus then answered, "That is the one for whom I shall dip the morsel and give it to him." So when He had dipped the morsel, He took and gave it to Judas, the son of Simon Iscariot. 27 After the morsel, Satan then entered into him. Therefore Jesus said to him, "What you do, do quickly."

14. What did Jesus know in these verses?

Don't miss this! Jesus knew what was coming. He knew the hour of His death was approaching. Jesus knew that the devil had entered into Judas.

15. According to verse 5 (on page 87), what did Jesus do?

Satan was waiting in the wings for his chance to enter Judas. Jesus knew it! And in the face of it, Jesus washed the feet of the one who would betray Him! Can you imagine such a thing? It is this kind of power that you have within you. The Holy Spirit gives the strength to love, even in the face of evil!

Foot washing is a display of humility and servanthood. It is an act of love and an example that we are to follow.

Read John 13:12-17:

12 So when He had washed their feet, and taken His garments and reclined at the table again, He said to them, "Do you know what I have done to you? 13 You call Me Teacher and Lord; and you are right, for so I am. 14 If I then, the Lord and the Teacher, washed your feet, you also ought to wash one another's feet. 15 For I gave you an example that you also should do as I did to you. 16 Truly, truly, I say to you, a slave is not greater than his master, nor is one who is sent greater than the one who sent him. 17 If you know these things, you are blessed if you do them.

We'd like you and your spouse to mirror this act of servanthood displayed by Jesus. Wash one another's feet. Don't overthink the preparations; simply pray together first for God to grow your love for one another through this act of service, commit yourselves to the Lord, and wash.

16. In question 11 we asked what surrender looks like in a marriage relationship. Have your thoughts changed or shifted in this matter? If so, how?

Journal Reflection

How did it feel to wash your spouse's feet? What have you taken away from this week's lesson?

Closing Thoughts

It can be so very difficult for us to surrender our selfish desires, our need to be right, our hurtful emotions, and our bitter responses to the Lord. But the same power that allowed Jesus to surrender, even to the point of death, to the Father's will lives within you. Jesus was so committed to His purpose that He was able to show humility and servanthood, even to the one who would betray Him.

Surrender is not a one-time thing. It is a decision that displays maturity and strength, not weakness and defeat, as the world would lead you to believe.

One final passage on surrendering for this lesson. Consider the instructions in these verses and how they relate to surrender. It is from James 1:19-21.

19 This you know, my beloved brethren. But everyone must be quick to hear, slow to speak and slow to anger; 20 for the anger of man does not achieve the righteousness of God. 21 Therefore, putting aside all filthiness and all that remains of wickedness, in humility receive the word implanted, which is able to save your souls.

Lesson 7
The Decision to Love

Lesson Introduction

The Decision to Love. It is the final decision we will study. And believe us, love IS a decision. The world has twisted and warped the concept of love. Phrases like "falling in love" or "love at first sight" or "you can't control who you love" or "I was made this way" make it seem like love is something that happens *to* us, and we have no control over it. We are innocent bystanders. Fate decides who we love.

We tell ourselves these lies—that you can't control who you love—so we don't feel accountable or have to take responsibility for the results of that love. After all, we were "meant to be together," right? It's not our fault?

Here is a hard truth: you **will** be held accountable for those you do and don't love.

Past Mistakes

Before we go further, it is important to note that God knows we have all made mistakes when it comes to love. We have made bad decisions. We may have been unfaithful in love. We may have hurt those we love and suffered tough consequences. This lesson might make you feel uncomfortable because of past sin.

Hear this word: if you have repented of that sin, God has forgiven you. If you have decided to do things His way, and no longer your way, He supports you and loves you. Any guilt you still carry can be cast off. If you've given the sin to Jesus, it's been forgiven.

The Choices of Love
Think back to the verses we studied in Lesson 5 from 1 Corinthians 13:

4 Love is patient, love is kind and is not jealous; love does not brag and is not arrogant, 5 does not act unbecomingly; it does not seek its own, is not provoked, does not take into account a wrong suffered, 6 does not rejoice in unrighteousness, but rejoices with the truth; 7 bears all things, believes all things, hopes all things, endures all things.

Paul's descriptions of love in these verses are all choices a person can make. We choose to be patient, we choose to be kind, etc.

In the Old Testament book Leviticus, God instructed the children of Israel:

17 'You shall not hate your fellow countryman in your heart; you may surely reprove your neighbor, but shall not incur sin because of him. 18 You shall not take vengeance, nor bear any grudge against the sons of your people, but you shall love your neighbor as yourself; I am the Lord.

The people were to choose to love their neighbors.

In Mark 12, in response to being asked of the greatest commandment, Jesus replied:

29 Jesus answered, "The foremost is, 'Hear, O Israel! The Lord our God is one Lord; 30 and you shall love the Lord your God with all your heart, and with all your soul, and with all your mind, and with all your strength.' 31 The second is this, 'You shall love your neighbor as yourself.' There is no other commandment greater than these."

God would not give us a command and then not equip

us with the power to see it through. If love was not a choice, we wouldn't be instructed to do it.

Where's the Passion?

In marriage, the concept of love gets muddied because sexual impulses or feelings of passion and attraction are also called feelings of love. We even call intercourse "making love." And when we say we "can't control who we love," often what we really mean is that we can't control who we are sexually attracted to. This, too, is a lie.

Hebrews 13:4 is pretty clear as to the sexual choices we are to make in marriage:

4 Marriage is to be held in honor among all, and the marriage bed is to be undefiled; for fornicators and adulterers God will judge.

Adultery is mentioned more than 50 times in Scripture, referring to both adultery in marriage and used as a description of idol worship against God. In all instances, it is abhorred. *"Thou shalt not commit adultery"* is even one of the Ten Commandments.

Adultery = clearly bad.

So as we move to our Scripture study, we will not focus on whether we can or can't control who we give our love to or whether we can or can't control our sexual desires. We will study how to passionately pursue our spouse so we are in unity and one with the Father.

The Spicy Meatball...
You can make the decision right now to love your spouse unconditionally for the rest of your life.

1. Do you agree with the Spicy Meatball statement? Are there any conditions you place on your love?

Me Time

A lifetime commitment to your spouse begins with the understanding that you are no longer two people living their lives in separate ways. You are one.

Read each of the three passages listed. As you read, consider what each one teaches about unity in marriage.

Genesis 2:22-25:
22 The Lord God fashioned into a woman the rib which He had taken from the man, and brought her to the man.
23 The man said,
"This is now bone of my bones,
And flesh of my flesh;
She shall be called Woman,
Because she was taken out of Man."
24 For this reason a man shall leave his father and his mother, and be joined to his wife; and they shall become one flesh. 25 And the man and his wife were both naked and were not ashamed.

Mark 10:6-9:
6 But from the beginning of creation, God made them male and female. 7 For this reason a man shall leave his father and mother, 8 and the two shall become one flesh; so they are no longer two, but one flesh. 9 What therefore God has joined together, let no man separate."

Ephesians 5:25-33:

25 Husbands, love your wives, just as Christ also loved the church and gave Himself up for her, 26 so that He might sanctify her, having cleansed her by the washing of water with the word, 27 that He might present to Himself the church in all her glory, having no spot or wrinkle or any such thing; but that she would be holy and blameless. 28 So husbands ought also to love their own wives as their own bodies. He who loves his own wife loves himself; 29 for no one ever hated his own flesh, but nourishes and cherishes it, just as Christ also does the church, 30 because we are members of His body. 31 For this reason a man shall leave his father and mother and shall be joined to his wife, and the two shall become one flesh. 32 This mystery is great; but I am speaking with reference to Christ and the church. 33 Nevertheless, each individual among you also is to love his own wife even as himself, and the wife must see to it that she respects her husband.

2. What do these passages teach about unity in marriage?

Read Philippians 2:1-3:

1 Therefore if there is any encouragement in Christ, if there is any consolation of love, if there is any fellowship of the Spirit, if any affection and compassion, 2 make my joy complete by being of the same mind, maintaining the same love, united in spirit, intent on one purpose. 3 Do nothing from selfishness or empty conceit, but with humility of mind regard one another as more important than yourselves;

3. According to these verses, how can we have unity?

Read John 17:22-24:

22 The glory which You have given Me I have given to them, that they may be one, just as We are one; 23 I in them and You in Me, that they may be perfected in unity, so that the world may know that You sent Me, and loved them, even as You have loved Me. 24 Father, I desire that they also, whom You have given Me, be with Me where I am, so that they may see My glory which You have given Me, for You loved Me before the foundation of the world.

4. Marriage relationships are to operate under the same love principles that Christ has for His church. According to these verses, what picture does Jesus paint for us? Draw below the image you have created in your mind as to how God, Jesus, and the Spirit exist together and where you and your spouse fit in the picture.

5. In what areas of your marriage do you and your spouse operate in unity really well?

6. In what areas are there room for improvement?

The biblical couple Hosea and Gomer are not often considered a shining example of a healthy marriage. But it is actually a beautiful picture of God's restoration. The Lord instructs Hosea (Hosea 1:2) to find a wife of harlotry, in other words, a prostitute, and Hosea is to have children with her. God uses Hosea's marriage to present an allegory for the unfaithfulness of the children of Israel. As Gomer runs after other men, Israel runs after other gods. Gomer breaks her marriage covenant, Israel breaks their covenant with God.

God allows Hosea to be the voice of prophecy for the Lord's promises and wrath. Hosea's marriage is a mirror to the pain and suffering caused when we break unity.

But there is hope.

Read Hosea 2:14-20, which speaks of the healing and peace that awaits.

"Therefore, behold, I will allure her,
Bring her into the wilderness

And speak kindly to her.
15 "Then I will give her her vineyards from there,
And the valley of Achor as a door of hope.
And she will sing there as in the days of her youth,
As in the day when she came up from the land of Egypt.
16 "It will come about in that day," declares the Lord,
"That you will call Me Ishi
And will no longer call Me Baali.
17 "For I will remove the names of the Baals from her mouth,
So that they will be mentioned by their names no more.
18 "In that day I will also make a covenant for them
With the beasts of the field,
The birds of the sky
And the creeping things of the ground.
And I will abolish the bow, the sword and war from the land,
And will make them lie down in safety.
19 "I will betroth you to Me forever;
Yes, I will betroth you to Me in righteousness and in justice,
In lovingkindness and in compassion,
20 And I will betroth you to Me in faithfulness.
Then you will know the Lord.

7. What hope do these verses hold for couples who may
have had their unity broken?

God is in the restoration business. He restores us to
Himself through Christ. He restores us to each other
through His lovingkindness and compassion. Just as Gomer
could not escape Hosea, you cannot escape God's eye. If
ever you stray, He awaits your return, and in His

faithfulness, He will pursue you.

When Hosea brings Gomer back home, he doesn't hold her harlotry against her. In Hosea 3:3 he tells her that he will be *toward her*, meaning, he will respect her and be kind to her. When seeking to restore unity, we, too, must make the decision to be *toward* one another, not holding sins against each other.

8. Are there things you might be holding against your spouse? Ask the Holy Spirit to reveal anything that may not be forgiven. Release them to the Lord so that complete unity can be restored.

We Time

The Song of Solomon is a book in Scripture like no other. On the eighth day of Passover, the Jews would sing portions of the Song of Solomon, a book they compared to the most holy place in the temple.[15]

The Song of Solomon is poetic, and reads as a call and answer between two lovers. In this **We Time**, you are going to read portions of the Song of Solomon to each other. Take note of the passion between the lovers.

Husband: (Song 4:1-6)
1 "How beautiful you are, my darling,
How beautiful you are!
Your eyes are like doves behind your veil;
Your hair is like a flock of goats
That have descended from Mount Gilead.
2 "Your teeth are like a flock of newly shorn ewes
Which have come up from their washing,
All of which bear twins,
And not one among them has lost her young.
3 "Your lips are like a scarlet thread,

And your mouth is lovely.
Your temples are like a slice of a pomegranate
Behind your veil.
4 "Your neck is like the tower of David,
Built with rows of stones
On which are hung a thousand shields,
All the round shields of the mighty men.
5 "Your two breasts are like two fawns,
Twins of a gazelle
Which feed among the lilies.
6 "Until the cool of the day
When the shadows flee away,
I will go my way to the mountain of myrrh
And to the hill of frankincense.

Wife: (Song 1:1, 16, 17, 2:3-6)
1:1 May he kiss me with the kisses of his mouth!
For your love is better than wine.
16 How handsome you are, my beloved,
And so pleasant!
2:3 Like an apple tree among the trees of the forest,
So is my beloved among the young men.
In his shade I took great delight and sat down,
And his fruit was sweet to my taste.
4 "He has brought me to his banquet hall,
And his banner over me is love.
5 "Sustain me with raisin cakes,
Refresh me with apples,
Because I am lovesick.
6 "Let his left hand be under my head
And his right hand embrace me."

Husband: (Song 7:1-4)
1 How beautiful are your feet in sandals,
O prince's daughter!
The curves of your hips are like jewels,

The work of the hands of an artist.
2 "Your navel is like a round goblet
Which never lacks mixed wine;
Your belly is like a heap of wheat
Fenced about with lilies.
3 "Your two breasts are like two fawns,
Twins of a gazelle.
4 "Your neck is like a tower of ivory,
Your eyes like the pools in Heshbon
By the gate of Bath-rabbim;
Your nose is like the tower of Lebanon,
Which faces toward Damascus.

Wife: (Song 7:10-13)
10 "I am my beloved's,
And his desire is for me.
11 "Come, my beloved, let us go out into the country,
Let us spend the night in the villages.
12 "Let us rise early and go to the vineyards;
Let us see whether the vine has budded
And its blossoms have opened,
And whether the pomegranates have bloomed.
There I will give you my love.
13 "The mandrakes have given forth fragrance;
And over our doors are all choice fruits,
Both new and old,
Which I have saved up for you, my beloved.

A marriage that mirrors God's holy romance is one in which you pursue your spouse with the passion and faithfulness that God has pursued you. It doesn't matter if you have been married for one, five, or thirty-five years, the pursuit should never end.

Just as you will continue to seek God more intimately until the day He calls you home, you must continue to go deeper and higher in your passion for your spouse.

9. Write words of affirmation or compliments to your spouse. What do you love about your mate? What about him or her makes your heart beat faster? What is your spouse's love better than?

Christians will sometimes work on their relationships with God with regular commitment, but forget to stay committed to their marriages. We go to Scripture to hear God's promises. We lay our hearts bare to God through prayer. We sing to and worship the Lord in our churches and in our private worship times. Do you take time to connect with your spouse on a deeper level? Do you affirm one another and show joy, simply because you belong to each other? Your spouse is not to replace God in any way, but God sees your marriage as extremely important. Do you?

10. Talk with your spouse. What is something you can do to connect with one another more deeply?

Journal Reflection

Look back at your pre-study questionnaire. Reflect on your responses. What has God shown you about yourself? About Himself? About your spouse?

Closing Thoughts

Remember what we said in the introduction: Satan hates your marriage. He knows the marriage relationship is a picture of the relationship Christ has with His church. He knows that the love we are to show one another is to be a mirror to the world of Christ's unconditional love for us. He knows if he can get a foothold in a Christian marriage, he can try and destroy your witness by breaking your unity.

But hear this: all Satan can do is tempt you. He cannot "make" you sin. You might feel like a rubber band that has been stretched to the limit and is just about at its breaking point, but you will not snap. God won't let you. He loves you and He loves your spouse too much. And He promises it:

No temptation has overtaken you but such as is common to man; and God is faithful, who will not allow you to be tempted beyond what you are able, but with the temptation will provide the way of escape also, so that you will be able to endure it. (1 Corinthians 10:13)

Nothing crushes Satan's plans with more force than when God's people show God's love to the ones Satan is trying hard to destroy.

Your marriage, as a picture of God's love, can draw others into salvation. When nonbelievers see you and your spouse handle life's problems with the love of Christ, they'll want to know, "How can you bear that?" When they see you pursue one another with the passion of Christ, they'll want to know, "How do you do it?" When you and your spouse make the decision that the way of the world will not be the way you do things, others will ask, "Why not?"

Your marriage can open doors to restore broken lives back to God, and more souls will be grafted into God's family tree of love. There is no greater privilege than being a part of someone else's salvation story. And when two are united in marriage and they make it their purpose to let their unity reflect Christ to a broken world... look out!

Friends, our purpose is not simply to avoid the evil in this world, but whenever possible to overcome it with His love. Consider it a blessing to do it side-by-side with the one you love. Till death do you part.

God loves you.

Questionnaire

Complete these questions prior to working on Lesson 1 of this study. You can keep these questions private; you will not be asked to share them.

1. What are you hoping God to show you through this study?

2. What challenges do you face that you need God to help you overcome?

3. What areas of your marriage are strong?

4. What area of your marriage needs growth?

Leader's Notes

You may have heard it said that if you make yourself available, God will give you the ability. A willing servant is a blessing to many. With your willingness to serve as a group leader, you commit to preparing before each group time. The leader sets the example for the group.

You don't have to be a biblical scholar to lead a small group. You do need a love for Jesus and the willingness to do your part. We pray these next pages will help you as you prepare for each small group gathering. Collectively, we have led hundreds of men and women through small group experiences. We have seen groups thrive and groups fail. In this section we'll provide you with some general tips, followed by session-specific notes.

GENERAL NOTES

- Be prepared. As mentioned above, the rest of the group may or may not complete the session work, but you need to set the example by being ready.
- Identify a back-up. Is there someone in the group who would be available to step up in case you have a sick child, emergency, or other problem arise at the last minute? Identify that person before the group even begins.
- If your small group includes snacks or food, give everyone a 2-minute warning to freshen coffee, get their plates, and find their seats before you begin.
- As the leader, be the one to open study time with prayer. If you are the one praying, then you have the

floor, and you can move right into the lesson
following your prayer.

- You are the guide, but the journey is about the group.
As such, each lesson includes a mix of discussion
questions with questions that can be learned right
from Scripture. Discussion about real-life gives
opportunity for discipleship.
- Ask a question, then be patient for an answer. If your
group is hesitant to answer a question, politely give
some space for the Spirit to prompt someone to
speak up. Don't rush in and answer your own
question.
- Do not force someone to talk if they truly do not want
to. It may have been a huge step of faith for someone
to even show up. Never bully someone into
answering a question.
- Bring it back to the Bible. Everyone has an opinion,
and we don't want to confuse our opinions with what
God says. Don't be afraid to say, "That's an interesting
viewpoint. Why don't we see what God says on the
matter?"
- Don't be afraid to shelf a question and tell someone
that you don't know the answer at the moment, but
you will see what the Bible says and will reply at the
next session. Remember, you aren't expected to know
everything. Don't answer something if you aren't
sure. Find an expert to help. (Pastor, trusted biblical
source, commentaries)
- Decide ahead of time the time frame and structure.
Don't work on the fly. Your group will appreciate
when you adhere to a schedule.
- Leave time for fellowship.
- End the official study time with prayer.
- Send an encouraging e-mail or text midway between
study gatherings, so members know you are thinking
about them. It may also prompt them to work on

their lessons.
- Ask God to show you what you need to know about those in your group. He has a purpose for you and for each one there. Ask Him to reveal it to you and be willing to engage with those He brings to you.

SAMPLE GROUP OUTLINE

This suggestion for your group time is based on our experience and this specific study.

1) Prayer.
2) Highlight anything from the **Lesson Introduction** that stood out to you. Read those portions out loud or paraphrase the introduction in your own words, sharing your experience on the topic.
3) Read the **Spicy Meatball** statement. Ask the group to share how the statement made them feel.
4) Use the Scripture Study Comments beginning on the next page to support your discussion on the **Me Time** questions.
5) Choose one or more of the **We Time** questions from that lesson's study. You also might have couples wait until the group time to do the We Time portion of the study. Be ready to give your own answers or an example to kickstart discussion if necessary.
6) Ask one or more of the following questions:
- What has God shown you this week that is new from His word?
- What stood out the most to you in this session's lesson?
- Did this lesson's study bring to mind any specific situations or experiences that maybe you haven't thought about in a long time?
- Did your thinking about the Spicy Meatball change

after going through the lesson? If so, how?
- Is there anything you've committed to God to do differently as a result of this lesson? If so, what?
- Was there anything in the content that was unclear or that formed new questions in your mind? What are they?

7) Close with prayer.

SCRIPTURE STUDY COMMENTS

Introduction

Encourage participants to complete the "Before you begin" questionnaire on page 105. This is for their eyes only; they don't need to share with you or their spouse if they don't want to.

This study is written with the assumption that both spouses are present and that both spouses want their marriage to be strengthened by biblical principles. We know this isn't the case for all marriages. This study, however, is intended for Christ-following couples. We suggest a gospel presentation and giving the opportunity for individuals to respond to the gospel in the first gathering of your small group.

There are three foundational truths presented in the introduction. Spend time talking about them to address any questions.

LESSON 1: The Decision to Be Different

The main point: The marriages of Christ followers are to be dramatically different from the marriages of those who live by worldly views of success. Living this out begins with the decision that when our spouse does something that evokes a negative emotional reaction, we will take a step back and listen for the voice of Jesus to say, "It is not to be this way among you."

The world fights for power, the Christ follower strives

for servanthood. The We Time this week allows space for real talk as to what the "fight for power" looks like in marriage. The decision to serve when we want to prevail is a difficult one. Couples may come to the table with a long history of each one fighting to get his or her way. Encourage participants not to dwell in the past. If one or another is angry over past power struggles in the marriage, ask them to consider what servanthood looks like "right now." We may not have acted with servanthood in mind in the past, but we can make better decisions NOW.

LESSON 2: The Decision to Pray

The main point: Prayer is the starting place for change. We cannot simply pray for other people to change, we must ask God for change in our own hearts. Places where we resort to coping mechanisms that don't involve God are areas we need to especially put the microscope on to see what God might want to change within us.

We saw in the verses from Acts that it is possible to rejoice, pray, and give thanks in all circumstances. Our own tough situations can be addressed with this "formula."

The We Time provides specific strategies and techniques for couples to use when praying. If you have couples who are new to praying together, encourage them to pick one technique to start with. Practice the techniques in class if you have time.

LESSON 3: The Decision to be Faithful

The main point: Faithfulness to your marriage is a product of your small, day-to-day decisions. Your emotional energy should be treated as a precious commodity, and your sexual energy is to be reserved for your spouse alone. You protect it by being ruthlessly discerning about the voices you allow to "speak" into your marriage, the things you allow your eyes to linger on, and by making the choice to seek God first, so that everything else will fall into line.

You support your spouse's spiritual needs by ensuring you are meeting your own. Then you are in the best position to meet the physical, emotional, and sexual needs of your spouse.

LESSON 4: The Decision to Trust

The main point: We are to place our trust in God alone. The world's ways will always lead to disappointment.

Even though we use the same word "trust" to convey what we believe about God and when talking about trusting man, the definitions behind those two situations should be very different. Trust in God is a deep belief in Him as a place of refuge, as a stronghold, as a foundation, as a solid truth. We are not to trust man (or things of the world) in that way. Our marriages should reflect God's love and be safe places. Any trust, or expectations, we place on our spouse should come from a godly perspective, not a worldly one.

We must make the decision to trust God's word as the truth we follow in our marriage.

LESSON 5: The Decision to Forgive

How does the statement Jesus makes in Matthew 18:35 and in Mark 11:25 sit with the members of the group? Is it a tough truth? We do not understand how great our own salvation is if we are unable to forgive others. We won't always get it right; but in increasing measures, we should find ourselves growing in mercy, compassion, and love for those around us. If we are not, then we really don't understand how big of a sacrifice Jesus made on our own behalf.

Spend time considering verses 4-7 in 1 Corinthians 13. You can ask spouses to talk together about which are easier and which are more difficult aspects of God's love to live out. Verse 5 instructs that love "does not take into account a wrong suffered." This means God's love is a forgiving love. We can't hide from that truth or put human parameters around it.

The lessons learned from Peter in Matthew 14 will help us when our human emotions threaten to overtake us. They give us tangible actions to take in tough times.

LESSON 6: The Decision to Surrender

The main point: To the world's eye, surrender is equated with failure. In God's economy, surrender is the beginning of victory in Christ. Making the decision to surrender to Christ happened at the moment of our salvation. But surrender isn't a one-time thing. It is a daily decision to lay down our selfish desires and put on God's love for others.

This lesson asks readers to reflect on their own salvation. Share salvation stories if possible.

Often we bristle at the word surrender because we see it as weakness. Jesus was anything but weak! In John 13 we read that Jesus took an attitude of servanthood and washed the feet of the one who only moments later would betray Him and hand Him over to death. Does this truth bring a new sense of humbling to anyone?

Jesus's death was torturous. He endured it willingly. There is no greater strength than that. When we embrace the magnitude of what Jesus did for us, and realize His power is within us through the Holy Spirit, we can stand up for anything. We can surrender in a position of powerful servanthood. We pray couples leave this session feeling empowerment through Christ.

LESSON 7: The Decision to Love

The main point: Love is a decision we make. We can decide now to love our spouse, no matter what.

When a marriage reflects God's holy romance, lives

are changed and lives can be saved. What a glorious motivation to pursue the truths in Scripture for our marriages.

This last session is one we hope sparks passion and fun in the marriage. Have couples do the "call and answer" of Song of Solomon with one another. Encourage them to write words of love and affirmation to each other. Send them out understanding that just as God pursues us into his holy romance, we should pursue our spouse with passion, commitment, faithfulness, and love.

Use this final group time to celebrate the new truths that each one has learned as related to their personal understanding of Jesus' love and marriage. If a couple has done even one of the lessons in the study, then we are confident that God has had a word to say to them.

Review or address any points you may have not gotten to because of time constraints, and celebrate any barriers that have been broken. In the pre-study questionnaire readers were asked what they hoped God would show them through the study. What did God show them?

End with prayer. We would love to hear your success stories and comments. Please share them with us!

About David and Kimberly

David Soesbee is an ordained minister. He has served the Lord as an evangelist for more than 25 years. Through his international speaking and teaching ministry, What Jesus Did, David connects with all age groups and cultures to share the message of salvation in Jesus Christ. David is the author of *What Jesus Did*, a Bible Study designed to equip believers how to share their faith without fear.

You can connect with David through his website:
www.WhatJesusDid.org
Twitter: @WJDMinistry

Kimberly Soesbee is an author and writing coach. She enjoys speaking and leading workshops, drawing from her experience as a mom, a former Division I athlete, a wife, and a woman seeking God's best. Her books include: *Maneeya, Made in Haiti, The Cookie Tree, Radical Love, Heartfish and Coffee* and more.

You can connect with Kimberly through her website:
www.KimberlySoesbee.com
Twitter: @AuthorSoesbee

REFERENCES

1 "Universal Emotions." Paul Ekman Group, 13 Nov. 2021, https://www.paulekman.com/universal-emotions/.

2 Cowen, Alan S., and Dacher Keltner. "Self-Report Captures 27 Distinct Categories of Emotion Bridged by Continuous Gradients." Proceedings of the National Academy of Sciences, vol. 114, no. 38, 2017, https://doi.org/10.1073/pnas.1702247114.

3 "New Marriage and Divorce Statistics Released." Barna Group, https://www.barna.com/research/new-marriage-and-divorce-statistics-released/.

4 Soesbee, Kimberly, and Donna Lowe. Examine Your Heart, Touch Publishing, Grand Prairie, TX, 2015, p. 5.

5 "Strong's Concordance." Greek Concordance: Ἀγανακτεῖν (Aganaktein), https://biblehub.com/greek/aganaktein_23.htm.

6 Soesbee, Kimberly, and Donna Lowe. Examine Your Heart, Touch Publishing, Grand Prairie, TX, 2015.

7 Rosner, Elizabeth. "US Divorce Rates Skyrocket amid Covid-19 Pandemic." New York Post, New York Post, 2 Sept. 2020, https://nypost.com/2020/09/01/divorce-rates-skyrocket-in-u-s-amid-covid-19/.

8 *QJM: An International Journal of Medicine*, Volume 113, Issue 10, October 2020, Pages 707–712, https://doi.org/10.1093/qjmed/hcaa202

9 Lehmiller, Justin J. "How the Pandemic Is Changing Pornography." Psychology Today, Sussex Publishers, 23 Mar. 2020, https://www.psychologytoday.com/us/blog/the-myths-sex/202003/how-the-pandemic-is-changing-pornography.

10 Loehr, Jim, and S. Tony. The Power of Full Engagement. Shubhi Publications, 2009.

11 "Strong's Concordance." Strong's Hebrew: 983. (Betach) -- Security, https://biblehub.com/hebrew/983.htm.

12 "Strong's Concordance." Strong's Hebrew: 539. (AMAN) -- to Confirm, Support, https://biblehub.com/hebrew/539.htm.

13 "Lewis B. Smedes Quotes." BrainyQuote, Xplore, https://www.brainyquote.com/authors/lewis-b-smedes-quotes.

14 Poe, Edgar Allan, and E. McKnight Kauffer. The Complete Poems and Stories of Edgar Allen Poe. A.A. Knopf, 1971.

15 Arthur, Kay, and John C. Whitcomb. The New Inductive Study Bible: Updated New American Standard Bible. Harvest House, 2000.

www.ingramcontent.com/pod-product-compliance
Lightning Source LLC
Chambersburg PA
CBHW061958040426
42447CB00010B/1801